CALLED AS WE ARE

BY ED NEELY

Copyright © 2016 HAYES PRESS. All rights reserved. No part of this book may be reproduced, stored in a retrieval system, or transmitted in any form, without the written permission of Hayes Press.

Published by:

HAYES PRESS

The Barn, Flaxlands

Royal Wootton Bassett

Swindon, SN4 8DY

United Kingdom

www.hayespress.org

First Edition August 2017

10 9 8 7 6 5 4 3 2 1

Unless otherwise indicated, all Scripture quotations are from the New American Standard Bible® (NASB®), Copyright © 1960, 1962, 1963, 1968, 1971, 1972, 1973, 1975, 1977, 1995 by The Lockman Foundation. Used by permission (www.Lockman.org). Scriptures marked RV are from the Revised Version Bible, 1885 (Public Domain). Scriptures marked KJV are from the King James Version, 1611 (Public Domain). Scriptures marked NKJV are from the HOLY BIBLE, the New King James Version® (NKJV®). Copyright © 1982 Thomas Nelson, Inc. Used by permission.

Table of Contents

CHAPTER ONE: CALLED AS WE ARE 1

CHAPTER TWO: LOVE YOUR NEIGHBOUR 6

CHAPTER THREE: TEMPTATION 12

CHAPTER FOUR: THE CITIES OF REFUGE AND THE CITIES OF THE LEVITES 14

CHAPTER FIVE: IN SPIRIT AND IN TRUTH 20

CHAPTER SIX: THE GLORY OF THE HOUSE 22

CHAPTER SEVEN: MOSES' WRONG ANSWER 27

CHAPTER EIGHT: A SEPARATED NATION 30

CHAPTER NINE: A LACE OF BLUE 35

CHAPTER TEN: IN THE SHADOW OF CALVARY 37

CHAPTER ELEVEN: THESE TEN TIMES 42

CHAPTER TWELVE: THE DAY SHALL DECLARE IT 44

CHAPTER THIRTEEN: PERSONAL WITNESSING 49

CHAPTER FOURTEEN: LIGHT IN THEIR DWELLINGS 54

CHAPTER FIFTEEN: THE SIN OFFERINGS 59

CHAPTER SIXTEEN: THE SWEET SAVOUR OFFERINGS 65

CHAPTER SEVENTEEN: THE SHEPHERD'S RODS 71

CHAPTER EIGHTEEN: PROPHETS OF REVIVAL! 74

CHAPTER NINETEEN: JEALOUSY 79

CHAPTER TWENTY: THE QUIET TIME 81

CHAPTER TWENTY-ONE: FURNISHED LIBERALLY 84

CHAPTER TWENTY-TWO: A CHOSEN RACE 86

CHAPTER TWENTY-THREE: QUAKE! 91

CHAPTER TWENTY-FOUR: HOLY LIVING 93

CHAPTER TWENTY-FIVE: GOSSIP 98

CHAPTER TWENTY-SIX: MAKING DISCIPLES 101

CHAPTER TWENTY-SEVEN: THE CHOSEN SERVANT 106

CHAPTER TWENTY-EIGHT: PRAISE IN PRAYER 109

CHAPTER TWENTY-NINE: CHRIST IN MATTHEW'S GOSPEL 114

CHAPTER THIRTY: THE ERROR OF MONARCHIANISM 117

CHAPTER THIRTY-ONE: SONS OF THE MIGHTY 121

CHAPTER THIRTY-TWO: MOSES THE MAN OF GOD - CHOSEN, PREPARED AND CALLED 123

CHAPTER THIRTY-THREE: CHOICES 127

CHAPTER THIRTY-FOUR: ON THE THRONE - GOD'S SOVEREIGNTY OVER THE NATIONS 128

CHAPTER THIRTY-FIVE: WHY THE EXCITEMENT? 133

CHAPTER THIRTY-SIX: GIVING TO GOD 135

CHAPTER THIRTY-SEVEN: BETHLEHEM 140

CHAPTER ONE: CALLED AS WE ARE

God doesn't think and do as we think and do, and clearly He does not think and do as we think He ought: "For My thoughts are not your thoughts, nor are your ways My ways," says the LORD. "For as the heavens are higher than the earth, so are My ways higher than your ways, and My thoughts than your thoughts" (1).

An example of a difference might be seen when God called Abraham to be a father of nations. He gave him a wife who was barren. Eventually, contrary to all nature, he had a son, Isaac, who also received a barren wife. Ultimately, however, Jacob was born. Jacob, Isaac's son, in turn, married a girl that he did not love and another whom he did, but who was also barren. Three barren generations, according to human wisdom, is hardly the way to propagate and populate a multitude of peoples and nations. We simply would not have done things that way! God's ways are not our ways!

Again in the New Testament when God desired to develop a people for Himself, a capable people endowed with wisdom and ability, He began with a very small group of very incapable, unlearned and seemingly undesirable men. Had the religious leaders and the rabbis of the time been garnering disciples, they would have chosen from the ranks of the ceremonially clean, the ones they thought righteous according to the Law, men of sufficient intelligence and interest to study the Torah, perhaps with a view to becoming rabbis themselves, certainly men who were examples to others, who could display sterling disciple qualities; (men whom John the Baptizer through the Spirit's wisdom called 'offspring of vipers' (2)).

Instead, Jesus, doing His Father's will, called to Himself a curious cross-section of contemporary society: down-to-earth and somewhat self-centred fishermen, more concerned with who was greatest among them than the Great One who walked in their midst; zealots who were in almost constant revolt against the Romans rather than those who were zealous for the things of God; a despised turn-coat tax collector suspected of fleecing rather than feeding God's sheep; and one other who seemed to rob them blind, whose end was destruction. Jesus' twelve disciples excluded His very own family, though after His crucifixion some are named as part of His people. His disciples had a mixture of Greek and Semitic names, perhaps a Judean along with Galileans, indicating a real microcosm of the Judaism of His day.

Nor, as we see, was this to be a unique choosing of disciples, as Paul reminded the Corinthian church: "For you see your calling, brethren, that not many wise according to the flesh, not many mighty, not many noble, are called. But God has chosen the foolish things of the world, "the weak things, the base things, the things which are despised, and the things which are not, to bring to nothing the things which are, that no flesh should glory in his presence" (3). The wisdom and nobility of this world might have been highly prized by those of Corinth and those like them of Greek and Roman origins who prized their wisdom, but again we are reminded of the vast differences between the ways of God and men. Not only is the word of the cross foolishness to those who are perishing, but God still uses those who might be considered foolish and of no consequence to convey His message, "fools for Christ's sake" (4).

It is not the brilliance, strength and nobility of man that can appreciate the plans of God, not human self-confidence, but self-effacing faith that opens for us the narrow way and an understanding of His Word that enables us to realize that we "have the mind of Christ" (5). If Christ had chosen His own followers on the basis of human wisdom and good breeding the twelve apostles, the heroes of the New Testament, as well as us might well have been passed by. Instead He chose the very ordinary, turning human understanding and the worldly way of thinking upside down, that He might do extra-ordinary things through His own to His glory and one day receive them - and others through them - into the glorious courts of heaven.

Not only were the unschooled and ignoble called to discipleship and the fellowship of the Son of God, but a long list of those possessed in earlier days of the grossest sins had been likewise called, washed, sanctified, justified in the name of the Lord Jesus and by the Spirit of our God (6), not because God had any affinity with iniquity, but to demonstrate His grace and mercy and to prove the efficacy of the sacrifice of Christ on their behalf. God has called the dead in transgressions to life in Christ and as those so called we glorify His name.

In the wisdom of God not only has the way of salvation been hidden from the wise and understanding and revealed to babes, but the path of the disciple as well seldom discloses to the unbeliever the glories that shall be and the peace we have now in our hearts. Even the Apostle Paul was considered foolish, was defamed in his ministry, dishonoured, disgraced, reviled, persecuted and considered the off-scouring of all things. He laboured at his own expense, and was sent out as Christ was sent out; a lamb in the midst of wolves, weak for the sake of the weak, a servant of men that his Master might be glorified and the gospel might flourish. At times even reviled among churches that should have known better, he suffered at the hands and tongues of his brethren. His day of acknowledgement and reward awaits God's soon-coming day of recompense.

God, like Paul, does not wish that His message be distorted by association with the things that are so prized by the wisdom of this world. Those things, which James describes as sensual and demonic, are the very antithesis of the wisdom that is from above, which is pure, peaceable, gentle, reasonable, full of mercy and good fruits, unwavering and without hypocrisy (7). All in the New Testament churches and we ourselves were called as we were;

> Just as I am, without one plea,
>
> But that Thy blood was shed for me,
>
> And that Thou bidd'st me come to Thee,
>
> O Lamb of God, I come! (8)

It has not yet been revealed what we shall be, but we know that when He is revealed, we shall be like Him (9). In the meantime we should strive daily to be more like Him here and now. That desire, rather than an undue striving to excel in the things of the world, is to be our aim (10). The Holy Spirit through the Word of God reveals what a balance in these things should be.

We are not, therefore, to continue in the behaviour and character in which we were called. We commence our discipleship as infants in Christ. Then we are taught and begin to grow. We find that the message of the cross which at first attracted us through the Spirit's gracious working contains more than justification. It concerns our sanctification; it concerns a renewal of attitude and action in response to the revelation of God; it calls for righteousness in thought and deed. It teaches us that the way to exaltation is humility and often humiliation, the way of obedience the way to the revealed wisdom of God.

Our involvement in this call by Christ is to an active rather than passive participation in what God has called us to, an inclusion in something amazingly and completely different from what is all around us. We actually talk to God and expect answers! We are invited to bring our praises right into His very sanctuary. We are welcome to discuss our individual concerns, but more than that, when as a people for God we present the fruit of lips making confession to Christ's name (11) we join with saints, angels, and heavenly beings, thrilling the heart of God with thoughts of His Son. Thanks be to God that we were called as we were! Thanks be to God that we are not now as we once were! Thanks be to God that there are even better things ahead!

References: (1) Is.55:8,9 (2) Matt.3:7 RV (3) 1 Cor.1:26-29 (4) 1 Cor.4:10 (5) 1 Cor.2:16 (6) 1 Cor.6:9-11 (7) Jas.3:15,17 (8) C. Elliott (9) 1 Jn.3:2 (10) 1 Cor.7:17,24 (11) Heb.13:15 RV

CHAPTER TWO: LOVE YOUR NEIGHBOUR

"Therefore, whatever you want men to do to you, do also to them, for this is the Law and the Prophets." (Matt.7:12).

Love Your Neighbour

Our text, this key verse from the Sermon on the Mount, concisely expresses the practical form that Christlikeness should take in our actions towards others. Its context, the inappropriateness of earthly anxiety, demonstrates the additional effect that its practice will have upon ourselves. The Lord had just finished telling His listeners that He had come to fulfil the law and the prophets. This summation of both of these, closely resembling the royal law of James 2:8, epitomizes His desire for the behaviour of all who would be sons of the Kingdom.

Leviticus 19:18 is quoted seven times in the New Testament, each time through its context revealing something further of the Person who fulfilled it, and giving further direction to those who would be His disciples: You shall love your neighbour as yourself. Matthew 5:44 adds the love of enemies; 19:21, responsibility to those less fortunate; 22:39, the impossibility of loving God without loving one's fellow. Mark 12:33 shows the superiority of love over sacrifices and offerings, while the quotation in Galatians 5:13-15 underscores its importance in our lives in fellowship with believers. Luke 10:25-37 stresses the necessity for action rather than passivity in its fulfilment, and James 2:8-9 shows how that fulfilment requires special care. Matthew 7 begins with the need for a correct estimation of the character of others and ends with a right estimation of God.

John also uses this order for the believer, while the unbeliever must firstly come to know God through Jesus Christ:

> "If someone says, "I love God," and hates his brother, he is a liar; for he who does not love his brother whom he has seen, how can he love God whom he has not seen? And this commandment we have from Him: that he who loves God must love his brother also" (1 Jn.4:20, 21).

> "Whoever believes that Jesus is the Christ is born of God, and everyone who loves Him who begot also loves him who is begotten of Him" (1 Jn.5:1).

Hurtful Criticism

If we are to be like Christ we must avoid being censorious: "Judge not, that you be not judged." This condemnation of others betrays the presence of hypocrisy in one's own life, a "beam" evidenced by a lack of love. The admonition against such judging, like the command to throw the first stone in John 8:7, redirects one's attention from the desire to correct or punish others to the need for personal repentance.

This doesn't mean that there is never the necessity to judge someone else. Indeed, the verses indicate that once a believer's own life is in order, he should remove the "mote" from his brother's eye, and Galatians 6:1 echoes the teaching that spiritual ones should aid in the restoration of those who have yielded to temptation. Furthermore, Matthew 7:16 give us the key to judgemental matters, saying, "You will know them by your fruits." But a critical nature uncontrolled develops bigotry and is most unbecoming of a disciple of Jesus Christ. Our progress is to be made through prayer (verses 7-11) not through criticism, a point about which preachers and writers need also to be reminded. And if this is true in our relation to non-believers, how true it is concerning those linked with us in the Kingdom. David's heart smote him after he had cut off part of Saul's robe while they were in the cave, David's hiding-place; so should ours when we attack in others the works and position of which such robes speak. "But if you bite and devour one another, beware lest you be consumed by one another!" says Paul (Gal.5:15).

> "Put on therefore, as God's elect, holy and beloved, a heart of compassion, kindness, humility, meekness, longsuffering; forbearing one another, and forgiving each other, if any man have a complaint against any ..." (Col.3:12,13).

The dual effect of this is outlined by Paul in Romans 14:

> "Therefore let us not judge one another anymore, but rather resolve this, not to put a stumbling block or a cause to fall in our brother's way ... For he who serves Christ in these things is acceptable to God and approved by men." (vv.13,18).

Moral discrimination is necessary, but it must work in conjunction with love, and whoever converts a sinner from the error of his way saves a soul from death and covers a multitude of sins says James (Jas.5:20). Peter joins the thoughts: "above all things have fervent love for one another, for "love will cover a multitude of sins" (1 Pet.4:8).

Don't Cast Your Pearls Before Swine

The covering of sins, however, does not give permission to the unbelieving to treat precious things as paltry. Neither dogs, nor those so-called in scripture (compare the use of dogs and swine in 2 Peter 2:22) have an appreciation of holy things; nor do swine value either pearls or those who offer them. "But the natural man does not receive the things of the Spirit of God, for they are foolishness to him; nor can he know them, because they are spiritually discerned" (1 Cor.2:14). What the natural man can see is the very practical translation of Christ and His word through our lives as we treat others as we would be treated.

Ask, Seek, Knock

Christlikeness will demand prayer. Peter reminds us of the Lord's attitude throughout His life here, culminating in His crucifixion, in all of which He left us an example that we should follow His steps: reviled, yet unreviling, threatened, yet unthreatening (1 Pet.2:21-23). But prayer is more than taking one's frustrations to the Father. In Luke's fourteen references to Christ in prayer there is not one hint of this. Indeed, He calls on His Father to forgive the very ones crucifying Him; and instructs the disciples to pray, forgiving others, that their own debts might be forgiven. Consistent and continuing communication with the Father is the very essence of Christlikeness. With due regard to the Greek tenses, Wuest amplifies verses 17,18 this way:

"Keep on asking for something to be given and it will be given you. Keep on seeking, and you shall find. Keep on reverently knocking, and it shall be opened to you. For everyone who keeps on asking for something to be given, keeps on receiving. And he who keeps on seeking, keeps on finding. And to him who keeps on reverently knocking, it shall be opened.

If we who are evil know how to give good gifts to our children, how much more does a heavenly Father know how to dispense good and unhurtful gifts?" The culmination of this, the supreme Good Thing given to His own is the Holy Spirit (Lk.11:13). It is significant that the "Golden Rule" verse comes where it does after the parenthetical account of prayer. What is more, the word therefore indicates that the good we do for others is to be patterned on what we have received from God. Alford says: "... give that which is good for each, to each, not judging uncharitably on the one hand, nor casting pearls before swine on the other."

That is, we do for others not what suits us, making ourselves and our tastes the standards by which others must receive, but rather we do what we might have reason to believe they would like to have done unto them. And this standard of behaviour is not to be used with the idea of obtaining for ourselves our own desires from another. The exhortation is not seen to be manipulative, either in Matthew 7:12 or in Luke 6:31. It is a guide, not a goal for one's actions: "Let each of us please his neighbor for his good, leading to edification. For even Christ did not please Himself" (Rom.15:2,3).

Nevertheless, God is debtor to no man. When Job prayed for his three friends so that they would not be judged according to their folly, God not only answered his supplication on their behalf, but also restored to him what he had lost, and doubled the amount. As we fulfil the royal law, there will be blessings which also accrue to our account down here. Christlikeness brings with it present as well as future blessings: love, joy, peace, patience, kindness, goodness; faithfulness, gentleness, self-control. It brings the security and fellowship that such qualities imbue, and reciprocal blessings coming from others who will react in kind to the Christian treatment accorded them.

Anxiety

On a very practical note, much of the anxiety that unfortunately at times characterizes human behaviour will disappear as we observe the Lord's teaching. Worry changes nothing but the worrier, and that not for the better. It can't change yesterday nor tomorrow; its only power is to rob the present of much of its potential. Be not therefore anxious, for though each day has its share of evil, this very practical Sermon on the Mount speaks blessing upon blessing to all who will seek first His kingdom, and His righteousness. In our doing as we would have done to us, we both glorify God and bring many benefits to the lives of others and our own.

Matthew 7:12, through its fulfilment of the law and the prophets has a parallel with the love commandments of Matthew 22:36-40. Our correct horizontal relationships, man with man, as we live as sons of the kingdom, must flow out of that great vertical relationship of love we have with God through our Lord Jesus Christ.

CHAPTER THREE: TEMPTATION

When believers are tempted they emerge from the temptation in two groups, the one much larger than the other. Temptation either leads to the fulfilment of our own lust, in turn conceiving sin and bringing forth death (Jas.1:15); or it strengthens our faith in God. Those who endure temptation are promised a crown of life (Jas.1:12). God gives us encouragement to meet each temptation with the knowledge that there is a way of escape.

Scripture teaches us all we need to know about temptation, concerning both the tempter and his methodology. A comparison of Genesis 3 with Luke 4 shows the scope of the trial: the tempting of body, spirit and soul with the lust of the flesh, and lust of the eye, and the vain glory of life. It also shows how to deal with its source. Eve desired the food of the tree for her body, delighted her eyes with it, and longed-for wisdom through it. She took and ate. The Lord Jesus Christ, tempted by Satan to satisfy His hunger by a miracle, denied His body: "Man shall not live by bread alone"; delighted not in the vision of worldly kingdoms: "Thou shalt worship the Lord thy God, and Him only shalt thou serve"; and rejected any temptation to act independently to His own glory: "Thou shalt not tempt the Lord thy God".

Every temptation is a variety of these. The scope falls well under the protection that God has provided for the believer. The power of the tempter pales under the pronouncement of God the Spirit who indwells us: "Resist the devil, and he will flee from you (Jas.4:7; 1 Pet.5:9). We know that we will be beset with temptation and the Scripture teaches us how to be victorious over it. We are not ignorant of Satan's devices.

Above all there must be the desire to overcome. We must not allow our minds to become sin's breeding grounds and then expect to be immune to its effects. Daniel's mind was skilled in all wisdom, endued with knowledge and understanding science, quick to be educated in language and custom, but all that together would not protect him in temptation. Daniel purposed in his heart that he would not defile himself. It was that purpose that brought about the proving of his faith through the threats of kings, pomp of power, plots of presidents, and mouths of physical and spiritual lions. In God's eyes he was a man greatly beloved, perfect and entire, lacking nothing (Jas.1:4), of whom the world was not worthy (Heb.11:32,38).

Purpose of heart will lead to separation of the godly from all that threatens to lead us in our own enticement and lust. Joseph's example is a good one for us all. Faced with temptation, he fled, and Paul exhorts us in his advice to Timothy to do the same: "Man of God, flee these things" (1 Tim.6:11; 2 Tim.2:22). Finally the armour of God will enable us to stand where flight is impossible. The victories of Josheb-basshebeth, Eleazar and Shammah (2 Sam.23:8-12) are won daily against far more dangerous foes by those who arm themselves as directed in Ephesians 6:10-18.

CHAPTER FOUR: THE CITIES OF REFUGE AND THE CITIES OF THE LEVITES

God's instruction concerning cities of refuge was no afterthought. It was given even before Moses had received the two tables of the law on Sinai, and was enlarged and repeated long before the land began to be conquered (Ex.21:12,13; Num.35:9-34; Deut.4:40-43; 19:1-13). These cities were to be established as part of the administration of a people for God's own possession and the direction concerning them was part and parcel of the statutes and commandments of the Lord basic to such a grand calling. As such, there are in that instruction counterparts appropriate to a called out and called together people for God in our own dispensation.

These cities and their teaching may of course be viewed as containing excellent illustrations of certain aspects of the grace of God to the sinner. Indeed, His grace to the sinner far exceeds the purpose of the cities of refuge, for it offers asylum to the guilty, something those cities could never do. However, our attention will concentrate on the view of those six cities as illustrations of God's provision for righteous judgement and justice among His people.

In both context and principle, the subject of the six cities is linked with an additional forty-two cities which were also given to the priests and Levites both as part of divine care for those wholly dedicated to spiritual service, and provision of a hands-on association between the exponents of the law of God and those who were to receive it. Because of Levi's wickedness, his father, Jacob, had foretold the scattering of his tribe in Israel away back in Genesis 49:7, but the goodness of God and the obedience of Levi in Exodus 32:26 overruled in this scattering being for the blessing both of the tribe and all the people.

Cities of Refuge

Four times in the book of Joshua the Holy Spirit adds special emphasis to matters discussed by introducing them with the words: "The LORD spoke (or said) to Joshua" (Josh.1:1; 4:1; 4:15; 20:1). The commission of Joshua, the setting up of the stones of witness, the removal of the ark from Jordan, and the instruction about cities of refuge have their importance underscored in this way. Whatever this meant to Israel, it becomes significant to us today as the teaching of these matters is applied to the present people of God.

It was never the purpose of God to hide sin, nor to make light of even the appearance of sin. There must be atonement made even for an unsolved murder, and local elders must be identified with a protestation of innocence as they washed their hands over the body of a heifer whose neck they had broken over a flowing stream in a valley in the murder area (Deut.21:1-8). A cleansing process was arranged, again through the sacrifice of a heifer, for a person who of necessity or involuntarily came in contact with a dead body or a grave. Association with death in any way was a defiling thing, and both the people and their land were defiled through the shedding of human blood. The intentional murderer must die. The accidental slayer, because there was neither hatred nor forethought involved in his action, was provided with a city of refuge. But even clear-cut cases of accidental death must come to trial before the elders of the slayer's own city.

The seriousness of bringing even accidental harm to another is demonstrated in that the slayer's own city was out of bounds unless this unwitting killer happened to outlive the high priest. From the date of his exoneration as a murderer, his freedom was limited by the walls of the city of refuge to which he had fled. No ransom could change his position, nor could money buy life for the man convicted of murder. The shedding of blood polluted the land, and this could not be condoned, for God dwelled in the land. No one must be condemned on the testimony of one person. Resident aliens, occasional travellers and citizens of whatever tribe were to be treated alike. God's justice is the same for all (Num.15:15).

These standards for God's Old Testament people have their lessons for the present for a people gathered together in grace. Then as now things become wrong or unclean because the Word of God so designates them in His sight, even in the absence of personal guilt. Old Testament principles and occurrences are recorded for our instruction that through perseverance and the encouragement of the scriptures we might have hope.

It would seem from Deuteronomy 19:11-12 that the elders of a man's own city were responsible to deal with the offender's case. He would of course have stated his case to the elders of the city of refuge to which he had fled (Josh.20:4): they would have granted asylum if there seemed to be a prima facie case for manslaughter rather than murder. In due course there would follow a hearing "before the congregation for judgement" (20:6), presumably in the man's home city.

If the verdict was manslaughter the congregation would send him back to the city of refuge to which he had fled (Num.35:24,25). If the verdict was murder the elders of his own city had the right to extradite him from the city of refuge and deliver him into the hand of the avenger of blood (Deut.19:12). Elders in both cities had their divinely given spheres of government and judgement. Yet they were responsible to cooperate in harmony with each other. They formed part of one national elderhood. In our own day also God has by His Spirit appointed elders to care for His flock (Acts 20:28). Paul writes to the Thessalonian church that they should appreciate men called to elderhood among them, and instructs these men also as to their care in guiding the flock of God:

> "Admonish the unruly, encourage the fainthearted, help the weak, be patient with all men. See that no one repays another with evil ... examine everything carefully ... abstain from every form of evil" (1 Thess.5:12-22).

The clearly written criteria of Scripture, whether then or now, provide the guidance for judgement. The elderhood is one throughout all the churches of God, and in matters of judgement there must still be cooperation and unity. If a brother is excommunicated from a church of God for wrong-doing, that judgement is upheld by all other churches of God throughout the Fellowship of churches. As sin in Israel polluted God's dwelling place, eventually occasioning His leaving the house (Jer.22:5; Matt.23:38), so unjudged and uncorrected sin in our own day must threaten the removal of His presence from His people (Rev.2:5; 3:16). Care to assure accuracy of testimony then and now is provided in the multiplicity of witnesses (Num.35:30, Matt.18:16, 2 Cor.13:1).

Cities of the Levites

To the six cities of refuge were added another forty-two cities (Num.35:6), and all forty-eight were to be given to the tribe of Levi: "As for the cities which you shall give from the possession of the sons of Israel, you shall take more from the larger and you shall take less from the smaller; each shall give some of his cities to the Levites in proportion to his possession which he inherits" (Num.35:8). This principle of giving is variously restated in the New Testament as a divine principle affecting God's care for those whom He has called to full-time service and for other purposes: "let each one of you put aside

... as he may prosper (1 Cor.16:2), and "... it is acceptable according to what a man has, not according to what he does not have" (2 Cor.8:12).

Under the Law of Moses proportional giving was never just an option, but it is possible and laudable to exceed Old Testament requirements in our own giving (Mk.12:43; 2 Cor.8:24). Noble Caleb demonstrates the attitude. Hebron had been both a promise and a long-standing dream to him, and when opportunity was finally given he claimed the area with his sword, in spite of giants and his own great age. Then much of that hard-earned precious territory he willingly gave back to God to be a city for the Levites and a city of refuge (Josh.14:7-13; 21:11-13). Its proximity to the temple and its great value made it a suitable city for Aaron's sons, the priests, who served in the courts of the Lord.

The tribe of Levi was without the inheritance that other tribes obtained, but the Lord who was their inheritance provided for their needs. No agricultural land was given to them, but pasture land surrounding their forty-eight cities was granted, perhaps a reminder both of the life which Israel had lived in the wilderness and of the nature of the shepherd care they must exercise as they moved among God's people teaching the doctrine of the Lord. Their basic income was the tithe of the nation (Numbers 18:20). The parallel is that those who proclaim the gospel get their living from it (1 Cor.9:7-14). The Levites, in turn, gave their tithe to the Lord for the priests (Num.18:28). These both might raise their own animals for meat and for sacrifice.

The accommodation of the cities did not belong to Levi exclusively, but they shared with others of the tribes in which the cities were found, and with the alien and traveller, and with the fleer to refuge. "Among which the Spirit of God has made you overseers, to shepherd ..." (Acts 20:28). As refuge was ever available, so also was the teaching of God to be near and available to all who would receive it. There was to be no partiality in this instruction, as Malachi 2:9 clearly shows. Yet the people being taught shared in the responsibility also: "For the lips of a priest should preserve knowledge, and men should seek instruction from his mouth, for he is the messenger of the LORD of hosts" (Matt.2:7).

God looked forward from Sinai to a day when Israel, beyond its wilderness wanderings would be at peace in the land of His promise. But further, He looked forward to our own day, granting in these instructions to Israel suitable teaching and illustration, for He dwells among a people now as then, and the basis of justice is God Himself, and the basis of His provision, His own beneficent character.

CHAPTER FIVE: IN SPIRIT AND IN TRUTH

They stood at the well together, the Samaritan woman who had known the rejection of human lovers, and the One who loved her with all the love of God. The Lord had to go to Samaria, itself a prompting of divine love (Jn.4:4). As well as offering her living water, He revealed to her a truth that has escaped so many: that the Father seeks worshippers who will worship in spirit and in truth (v.23). The phrase rolls off our tongue so often. What did the Lord Jesus really mean?

The word 'spirit' here does not refer to the Holy Spirit. Indeed we would be quite incorrect to imagine that others were not moved by the Holy Spirit in their worship or that our worship was any more in the Spirit than the sweet words of David or Asaph or Ethan. Worshipping 'in spirit' here is different from the truth of worshipping 'by the Spirit' (Phil.3:3). Nor is it simply conveying that a person must feel what he is saying in his own spirit; a step beyond merely voicing the praise with affirmation. This is not to deny, however, that in worship there is communication between our spirit and the Spirit of God (Lk.1:47). Before confirming what the Lord was positively saying here, we need to also consider His other characterization of worship as being 'in truth'.

There is a difference between "truth" and "the truth". The truth equates with the faith (Jude 3). These comprise the rules of the new covenant, just as the law had embodied the laws of the old covenant ratified at Sinai. Truth very often is simply the opposite of lies, but not in this case. It can also refer to that which is real and substantial over against that which is merely shadowy or typical.

So what was the Lord saying to this Samaritan whom He wished to enlighten? In spirit, here, is the antithesis of material ordinances, such as offerings and sacrifices, a mere shadow of good things to come. In particular, the Lord was indicating that physical venues at specific geographical locations would no longer be the important factor. Consistent with that, in truth is opposed to in type and shadow, which things merely pointed the way to better things prepared for us in a new covenant relationship. No longer are God's requirements written upon tables of stone, nor yet on whatever the Samaritans envisioned on Mount Gerizim. Instead they are written on fleshy tables of the heart, by the Spirit of God using His Word to direct us (Heb.8:10).

The English word worship is from the Middle English worthship, and means the acknowledgement of the object worshipped. Our worship in a collective mode is a declaration of the worth of Christ, not with material objects or with the things in a physical house, but among living stones built up as a spiritual house for 'a holy priesthood, to offer up spiritual sacrifices, acceptable to God through Jesus Christ' (1 Pet.2:5). When the Lord made His double antithesis (in spirit and in truth) with the material shadows of old covenant worship, He was heralding the dawning of a new era in which the essential factor would be a spiritual appreciation of the true nature of worship by disciples of Christ world-wide yet associated in a spiritual house.

The woman at the well may not immediately have grasped what the Lord meant. Do we?

CHAPTER SIX: THE GLORY OF THE HOUSE

"Beautiful in elevation, the joy of the whole earth, is Mount Zion in the far north, the city of the great King. God, in her palaces, has made Himself known as a stronghold" (Ps. 48:2,3).

The gem, the crown jewel, in the midst of a setting enhanced by all the riches of David and Solomon, was the house of gold, the house of God. The scene could only properly be viewed from the top of the Mount of Olives, and it must have shimmered in breath-taking splendour in the morning sun. Not only was it a joy to any who beheld it, as the sons of Korah intimated in this 48th Psalm, the third in a trilogy of God's refuge and Kingship, but it was a joy to the God who made Himself known in it (1 Kin.9:3). Seven years was Solomon in building it with the dedicated labours of hundreds of thousands skilled in their trades (1 Kin.5:6,13-16) and, more importantly with the divine stamp of the written directions of God handed to him by David, his father. It was erected at Moriah, the area where Abraham had raised an altar of burnt offering to sacrifice his son, and where David, hundreds of years later had purchased the threshing floor of Araunah. These associations seem appropriate to the location of the Temple. In the seven years of building it became the perfection of beauty.

Like the spiritual house of which it was a shadow, the stones of the structure were formed at the quarry and then built quietly into a dwelling place for God. Those living stones which are built together in God's spiritual dwelling today are formed and shaped at Calvary. It seems clear from 1 Chronicles 29:4 that silver had a part in covering the walls. Beams and planks of cedar covered the stone, so that an excellent unity was observed within and without rather than the prominence of each individual piece (1 Kin.6:18). Like the city of which it was a part, it was compacted together in a unity.

Unlike the former shadow, the Tabernacle in the wilderness, the structure in the land portrayed the willingness of God to reveal Himself. Whereas the Tabernacle whose structure and inner parts were largely unseen, whose beauty was largely hidden, and whose service depicted the approach to God of a people through a holy priesthood, the Temple radiated outside much of the glory that was within. Emphasis was placed on cherubim that looked out, as well as those which looked down. Twelve oxen, bearing the brazen sea faced outwards in all four directions also. Outer as well as inner carvings of cherubim, open flowers and palm trees adorned the cedar, and outside as well as inside was burnished with the gold of Parvaim. Though the common man was not allowed within that which was so holy, he could appreciate much of the inside beauty revealed in that which could be seen.

The very finest of materials went to build the temple, for it was a type of something most precious in the sight of God. Even nails, hinges and fastenings were of pure gold. From the Temple, in a very special way, was fulfilled the Psalm of Asaph: "The Mighty One, God, the LORD has spoken ... out of Zion, the perfection of beauty, God has shone forth (Ps.50:1,2). The Temple was the centre of the beauty of Zion. Everything was overlaid with gold, and in the gold were set precious stones (2 Chron.3:6). In the same way in a later spiritual dwelling, those who become partakers of the divine nature (2 Pet.1:4), have a collective opportunity of displaying that nature to all around, and the special God-given gifts which enhance His habitation display some of the essence of Him who conceived its structure and died for its purchase.

The queen of Sheba was awe-struck at the edifice and its entrance, the service and the evident expression of the wisdom of Solomon seen in all that pertained to the house of God. But she saw only the outside, and perhaps little appreciated that there was much more than human acuity at work here. The infinite majesty of the God of heaven disclosed something of itself within these walls and the service of a priesthood far excelled anything seen by earthly eyes. Only the ark of the covenant remained as it had been in the Tabernacle. The magnificence of the fifteen-foot tall, finely carved, gold-burnished, olive wood cherubim, the many golden lavers and lampstands of gold (and of silver), the ten tables, and all the basins, shovels, tongs were new, and made all of pure gold, gleamed in their magnificence, but their beauty was secondary to their holiness. "Holiness befits Thy house, O LORD, forever" (Ps.93:5).

In the porch of the house stood two great pillars of bronze, adorned with chains bearing bronze pomegranates, and topped by two magnificent capitals. These guarded the door to the house, and in their names, Jachin and Boaz, they bore silent testimony to the establishing strength of God who sat above the mercy seat. Pillars in God's house in any age exhibit the same strength, glory, fruitfulness (Rev.3:12). "And in His temple everything says, 'Glory!'" (Ps.29:9). Its cost was immeasurable, yet beggared by the cost of the house of which it spoke (Acts 20:28).

During the Feast of Booths in the seventh month of the seventh year of its building, the ark was brought in and "the glory of the LORD filled the house" (1 Kin.8:11). According to God's gracious answer to Solomon's prayer of dedication, the Temple would be the centre of God's affection and attention. "For now I have chosen and consecrated this house that My name may be there forever" (2 Chron.7:16), was the divine word that wrought more value to the Temple than all the earthly riches that were poured into it. God highly esteemed that house, so much that man also, giving it a high estimation, would know blessings abundant, even a fulfilment of the broad supplication of Solomon "as he stood before the altar of the LORD" (1 Kin.8:22-53). The instruction of Moses concerning that feast of the seventh month was that the people should be altogether joyful. Never had the people more reason to experience this: "On the eighth day he sent the people away and they blessed the king. Then they went to their tents joyful and glad of heart for all the goodness that the LORD had shown to David His servant and to Israel His people" (1 Kin.8:66).

God's high value of the vessels of the house is perhaps seen best as they are enumerated in Jeremiah 52:17-23 and in the post-exilic record in Ezra 8:25-30. Their holiness had been attested to by God at the feast of Belshazzar (Dan.5). Isaiah assures us that those who had to do with such holy things were also to be purified (Is.52:11). This house in all its grandeur, although it was a nation's showplace, was so much more than that. Solomon readily acknowledged that even the heaven and the heaven of heavens could not contain the One who deigned to dwell there (1 Kin.8:27), yet his God-appointed wisdom also revealed that this house was central to all God's purposes with the separated nation that God had called out from all the people of the earth as His inheritance (1 Kin.8:53). God's desire for His chosen people then, is reflected in Paul's prayer for His peculiar people of the moment: "I pray that the eyes of your heart may be enlightened, so that you may know ... what are the riches of the glory of His inheritance in the saints ..." (Eph.1:18).

The Temple in Jerusalem was to be a revelation of some of the power and majesty of the God of the house; so His people today are to proclaim the excellencies of Him who has called us out of darkness into His marvellous light (1 Pet.2:9). David died before the building of the temple that he had saved and sacrificed for, but his expression of appreciation for the place of the Name must have found place in the hearts of many in Israel as they contemplated the centre of divine activity, just as it reflects our own thought of God's spiritual house today: "O LORD, I love the habitation of Thy house, and the place where Thy glory dwells" (Ps.26:8) and: "One thing I have asked from the LORD, that I shall seek: that I may dwell in the house of the LORD all the days of my life, to behold the beauty of the LORD, and to meditate in His temple" (Ps.27:4)

CHAPTER SEVEN: MOSES' WRONG ANSWER

We hesitate to speak ill of Moses, a man of whom the Holy Spirit records great praise:

> "Now the man Moses was very meek, above all the men which were upon the face of the earth". "My servant Moses ... is faithful in all Mine house: with Him will I speak mouth to mouth ... wherefore then were ye not afraid to speak against my servant, against Moses?" (Num.12:3-8).

Yet the Spirit of God records some low points in the great man's career, things written aforetime for our learning. The Exodus 4 account of that great day on the far side of Sinai was one of them. Moses had been called into the presence of God-who revealed Himself as Jehovah, the I AM. He had been given one of the greatest commissions ever entrusted to man, to bring release to men and women in bondage and to lead them on to become the people of God. "And Moses answered and said, 'But...'"

A certain reticence in acceptance of divine recognition for higher service is a seemly thing, often in keeping with the character of the men God chooses for His great work. Gideon's appreciation of his family's position in Manasseh and his own place within his father's house was the kind of humility that helped to make him an illustration of a greater Saviour. Jeremiah's awareness of his own lack of development and fitness for his great service on behalf of God's people made him more reliant upon the One who said, "I am with thee." In neither case, however, nor in any case, is there room for argument against the call of God; no room for "But".

Peter made a similar mistake on that housetop in sunny Joppa. As in his vision the great sheet descended, and all manner of four-footed beasts and creeping things and birds were offered for him to kill and eat, he said, "Not so, Lord." His response to the command bespoke a life of exemplary dedication to the laws of God. "I have never eaten anything that is common and unclean". The three-fold lowering of the sheet was to remind Peter of another refusal when on a dark night he had thrice refused to acknowledge his Lord. With that still full in his memory, though forgiven, he had been ashamed to fully declare his love as the Lord persisted with the question, "Lovest thou me ...?" Yet all are called to divine service must learn that past error must not rob God of present service. There is no place for argument against Him, no "Not so" if there is to be a full acknowledgement of His Lordship. "Why call ye me, Lord, Lord, and do not the things which I say?" (Lk.6:46).

If anyone is called to divine service, whether through revelation of the Lord's will through His Word, or through recognition by his brethren, there may well be a feeling of unworthiness and insufficiency, but there should never be a "But" or "Not so". In some cases there may even be a hidden impediment in the life, some action or habit not brought under captivity to the obedience of Christ. Yet we all, even in fruitbearing, need cleansing, that we may bear more fruit.

Let us not allow natural reticence or sinful impediment to deter our service for the Master, for He has called us into His presence, knowing all our secrets and fears. He has revealed Himself to us, and desires to reveal Himself in us. He has given us the Great Commission to lead men out of bondage and to minister to them till they attain to the unity of the faith and of the knowledge of the Son of God, unto a full-grown man, unto the measure of the stature of the fulness of Christ. Christ has pledged Himself to be with us. Let us learn this lesson from the life of Moses, that we answer not with the "but" of disagreement, but with

Paul's willingness on the road to Damascus, "What shall I do, Lord?" (Acts 22:10).

CHAPTER EIGHT: A SEPARATED NATION

Pharaoh spoke the truth when he first refused to allow the separation of Israel when Moses requested it. "I do not know the LORD ..." Separation and holiness are part of the essential character of God and are enjoined upon all who know Him; those who do not know Him will find the ideal not only intolerable, but impossible (1 Pet.1:16; Heb.12:14).

The principles of separation are taught from Genesis 1 to Revelation 22; holiness is first mentioned in relation to the calling out of a people for God. As God called Moses for the task of leading out this people, He set the standard by allowing Moses to stand on holy ground, but only on the basis of Moses emptying himself of self and personal authority, and giving complete obedience to the command of God (Ex.3:5). God's self-revelation to and in a nation demanded their separation: "Let My people go, that they may serve Me ..." What was true of Israel is also true today of a nation called out of darkness into light. He who rejects that separation, answers in the same measure as Pharaoh, "I do not know the Lord".

The Bible states ten times that Pharaoh hardened his heart, and ten times that God hardened it. But God waited until the king had hardened his own heart seven times before He first hardened it, though God in foreknowledge had predicted that this would be so. Indeed, God had raised him up so that divine power might be demonstrated in him (Rom.9:17). Yet the fact remains that it was in hardness of heart that Pharaoh rebelled against the purposes of God. Hardness of heart still wars against the separation that God desires for His people.

Pharaoh's claims that sacrifice is laziness, and that the miracles of men could explain away the miracles of God, couldn't convince even his own people (Ex.8:19; 10:7), yet he continued in his lies, mock-repentance and bravado, and decided that compromise must be the eventual answer. Poor Pharaoh - there is no compromise with God. Had Israel learned this earlier, they too might have been spared much of their torment under Pharaoh's hand (Ezek.20:8): Israel's idolatry in Egypt showed their unwillingness to trust God completely: "Then I resolved to pour out My wrath upon them, to accomplish My anger against them in the midst of the land of Egypt." The believer in Christ will also greatly benefit from learning that same lesson early.

The fact that God had made a division between the Egyptians and the children of Israel in the land of Egypt (Ex.8:22ff), was not sufficient reason to compromise by sacrificing to God within the land (Ex.9:25,26). Apart altogether from the obvious, that such sacrifices could only be misunderstood and obnoxious to the Egyptians, God had commanded the separation of His people (Ex.8:26,27). Present day collective service demands a similar type of separation (Heb.13:12-15).

The prophecy of Hosea 11:1, fulfilled in Christ (Matt.2:15), still calls for obedient response in the hearts and lives of those who would live godly lives: "Out of Egypt I called My Son". Nor would separation with strings attached answer the command. "Don't go far away" (see Ex.8:28), is still the cry of a world that has yet to learn that righteousness and lawlessness have no partnership; light and darkness no fellowship; Christ and Belial no harmony. "Come out from their midst and be separate" says the Lord. "And do not touch what is unclean; And I will welcome you. And I will be a Father to you, and you shall be sons and daughters to Me" (2 Cor.6:14-18).

Not far away? The command to separate from, and separate to, is total and absolute. That only some should go, or that possessions be left behind, must be answered with resolve and fulfilment: "not a hoof will be left behind". Furthermore, when God brought them out they would not go empty. The night of their separation is described as "for the LORD" (Ex.12:42). He would bring them out and bring them in full. Their continuation in that fulness and the enjoyment of it would depend on continued political, connubial, and ecclesiastical separation.

Today, right thinking believers in the Lord Jesus Christ have no difficulty in seeing the necessity for separation from the grosser evils of this world. Difficulty sometimes arises, however, in discerning the need for separation in areas where we could seemingly benefit or be a benefit - politics, marriage, religious affiliation. The warnings of Deuteronomy 7 are the claims of God, not Moses: "For you are a holy people to the LORD your God; the LORD your God has chosen you to be a people for His own possession out of all peoples who are on the face of the earth ... Therefore, you shall keep the commandment and the statutes which I am commanding you today, to do them" (vv. 6,11).

No covenants, no favour in judgement, no intermarriage, no trying to reform the wrong religious worship - separation was to bring spiritual, physical, economic blessing beyond anything that they could imagine; less than separation would cause the nation to perish (8:19). God's standards have not changed in our dispensation. We are in the world and submissive to its authorities (Jn.17:15-18; 1 Pet.2:13-17), yet not of it and its ambitions and pleasures. Not only so, but spiritual enlightenment is a progressive thing and does not allow of a return to a degree darkness which at the time meant a measure of light to us: "For if I rebuild what I have once destroyed, I prove myself to be a transgressor" (Gal.2:18).

We never cease to be one with fellow members of the Body of Christ, but separation from practices inconsistent with the revelation of divine truth to us is ever taught in the New Testament, and involves separation, therefore, from people who are believers also. In the ultimate, this may even necessitate separation from some who are within our own churches as censure and discipline are carried out according to divine directions (Rom. 16:17;1 Cor.5:11; 2 Thess.3:6). Separation in itself does not involve enmity as 2 Thessalonians 3:14,15 clearly shows. This was illustrated in Israel's experience in Deuteronomy 2:5,9: Israel were brothers with Edom and Moab and were not to be jealous of God's blessings upon them nor envious nor covetous of their possessions. Israel turned away rather than engage in battle with them and took the long way around rather than vex those who also had received God's blessings. God would later show the principle - them that are without, God judges (1 Cor.5:13).

Balaam, with eyes wide open, enlightened by the Lord, saw God's vision of His people: "As I see him from the tops of the rocks, and I look at him from the hills; Behold, a people who dwells apart, and shall not be reckoned among the nations (Num.23:9). Who among God's people would have it otherwise? Isaiah says: "The nations are like a drop from a bucket, and are regarded as a speck of dust on the scales ... All the nations are as nothing before Him, they are regarded as less than nothing and meaningless" (Is.40:15,17).

But: "you are a chosen race, a royal priesthood, a Holy Nation, a people for God's own possession ... you are the people of God" (1 Pet.2:9-10). The importance of the nation that God chooses is underscored in the remarkable words of Deuteronomy 32:8,9: "When the Most High gave the nations their inheritance, when He separated the sons of man, He set the boundaries of the peoples according to the number of the sons of Israel. For the LORD's portion is His people." And: "Christ Jesus ... gave Himself for us, that He might redeem us from every lawless deed and purify for Himself a people for His own possession ..." (Titus 2:14).

A promise of blessings and curses followed God's call to Israel, each dependent upon the measure of obedience of the people to God's commandments. The checkered history of the nation proved the accuracy of divine promise. The history of God's dealings with the early churches of the New Testament is a re-statement of God's fidelity to His word. God will not be unfaithful to His word in our day either. Holiness and separation will bring blessing; and hidden manna, a white stone, and a place on the throne of Christ are still offered to the overcomer (Rev.2:17; 3:21). And to such as are otherwise, the promise of tribulation and pestilence and a spewing from the mouth of God. God's will is to dwell among a separated and holy people; a people who in every sense of the word "know the Lord":

> "I will dwell in them and walk among them; and I will be their God, and they shall be My people. Therefore, come out ... and be separate ... perfecting holiness in the fear of God (2 Cor.6:16-7:1).

CHAPTER NINE: A LACE OF BLUE

We don't know what motivated the man in Numbers 15 to gather sticks on the sabbath. Whatever the reason, it stood in direct opposition to the commandment of Jehovah. "Ye shall keep the sabbath therefore; for it is holy unto you: everyone that profaneth it shall surely be put to death". "Ye shall kindle no fire throughout your habitations on the sabbath day" (Ex.31:14; 35:3). So the whole congregation stoned him to death, as Jehovah commanded Moses. It is in this context that we are introduced to the meaning of the lace of blue. The wording is unique, a plea rather than a commandment:

> "Speak unto the children of Israel, and bid them that they make them fringes in the borders of their garments ... and that they put upon the fringe of each border a cord (lace) of blue ... that ye may look upon it, and remember all the commandments of the Lord and do them; and that ye go not about after your own heart and your own eyes ...."

The lace of blue was a reminder to obey. Where had they seen this before? "And they shall bind the breastplate by the rings thereof unto the rings of the ephod with a lace of blue, that it may be upon the cunningly woven band of the ephod, and that the breastplate be not loosed from the ephod" (Ex.28:28). Further:

> "And thou shalt make a plate of pure gold, and grave upon it, like the engravings of a signet, HOLY TO THE LORD. And thou shalt put it on a lace of blue, and it shall be upon the mitre; upon the forefront of the mitre shall it be. And it shall be upon Aaron's forehead, and Aaron shall bear the iniquity of the holy things".

What Aaron wore pictures the work of the Lord Jesus Christ in His High Priesthood. Through His obedience the Lord fulfils His calling. "Though He was a Son, yet learned obedience by the things which He suffered; and having been made perfect, He became unto all them that obey Him the author of eternal salvation; named of God a High Priest after the order of Melchizedek" (Heb.5:8-10). So He bears His people upon His heart and ensures the holy character of the gifts they offer, for He, too, bears the iniquity of the holy things. Should not the obedience of the High Priest be reflected in the people over whom He officiates? Should not the lace of blue be found in their lives as well as His? The lace of blue has a very real lesson to us all about obedience.

When all the wise-hearted of Israel constructed God's house at Sinai, they completed the ten curtains, five and five according to the pattern, then bound them into one with clasps of gold (Ex.36:8-13). These clasps that bound them into a unity were coupled together with loops of blue. What appeared in the garments of the High Priest appeared in the clothing of those that did God's bidding, and perhaps it is this that is seen in that which binds the house together. Certain it is that in our own day unity will be achieved in no other way.

The Lord's prayer included these words: "That they may be one, even as We are one; I in them, and Thou in Me, that they may be perfected into one" (Jn.17:22,23). We live in a world where circumstances pressure towards a life of disobedience. The example and bidding of the Lord is to obedience, that we follow not after our own way, but after all His commands.

CHAPTER TEN: IN THE SHADOW OF CALVARY

In a sense, the whole of eternity sits in the shadow of Calvary. Never was there, nor will there be, a more important event than the shedding of the blood of Christ, who through the eternal Spirit offered Himself without blemish unto God. Calvary is the fulcrum of human history, prophesied in early Genesis; central to the whole of Scripture, even the future in Revelation; and to the theme of praise and worship in the present, both here and in heaven. But here we look at the time just before what took place at Calvary.

By the weekend of that entrance into Bethany, the sixty-nine weeks of Daniel's prophecy (Dan.9:25) had all but run their course, after which Messiah was to be cut off. 483 years previously, Artaxerxes' command to rebuild Jerusalem (Neh.2:6) had excited the builders from Babylon to return. Since Peter's declaration that no matter what men in general thought, Jesus is the Christ, the Son of the living God, Jesus had been showing His disciples that He must go up to Jerusalem and suffer, and be killed, and be raised up the third day (Matt.16:21). Then He left Galilee for the last time, not to return there until after His resurrection. Now, this final week brings the culmination of all that these other things led up to, the fulfilment of divine purpose in the incarnation. It is not our purpose to attempt a harmony of the Gospels for this final week, save to reflect that all the Scriptures are true, and if hard for us to place in time sequence, it is we, not they, who are at fault. We shall confine our thought to matters recorded in John, the which have particular import when viewed in relation to their proximity to the death of the Lord Jesus Christ.

There may be some fruitful comparison between the specific days that began the ministry of Christ that are mentioned in the first two chapters of John and the six days that are outlined here at the end of His ministry in John 12-17. Certainly He did some things in those early days which are repeated here: His baptism and its counterpart in His death; the cleansing of the temple; and His appearing at a special dinner. Indeed, there seems to be a development worthy of note in the meals that He is recorded to have attended in this Gospel. At Cana He began as guest; in John 12:1 He is guest of honour; on the beach in John 21 He is the host. Our own lives would show growth if we allowed Him the same progress in them. As John said, "He must increase, but I must decrease".

The Bethany supper is the first mentioned opportunity for us to see the reunited family together after the resurrection of Lazarus. One notices the great similarity between the activities of that lovely trio before and after that occasion. Martha served; Mary sat at His feet; Lazarus, His friend, sat at table with Him; all graphically depicting a truth that is elsewhere emphasized in Scripture; our position and service after resurrection will be related to that which we have developed in life (cf. Matt.19:27-30; Matt.25:21; Lk.19:24; 2 Tim.2:11). Often throughout their lives would those gathered at that meal remember their fellowship with the Master, and many a time, no doubt, would the sweetness of that remembrance lighten the burden of the moment.

More than once in His lifetime had the Lord been anointed with precious perfume, and each occasion recorded (perhaps there had been many more) is rich in its teaching. But this anointing by Mary takes on a special significance because of its timing. Mary loved her brother Lazarus, yet that precious spikenard had not been used on his body, so recently dead. It was the anticipation of the Lord's burial that caused the sweetness to flow. Mary seemed to have an insight into the matter beyond even that of His apostles - perhaps gained in her hours spent at the Lord's feet. But her action was more than anticipatory. Mary identified herself with both His death and burial, not only by anointing Him, but by wiping His feet with her hair. It may have been a most unconventional thing for a Jewish woman to loose her hair in the presence of men, but convention gave place to devotion, and the whole house was filled with the fragrance.

There was to be no shortage of ointments and spices for His burial. Much of it, because it was brought too late, would never be used for the purpose. Yet a seeming surfeit of sweetness is no reason for not bringing the gift, a point underscored by the Lord's stout defence of Mary's action. His statement about the lasting nature of the matter, that it would be told wherever the gospel would be preached worldwide, shows the importance He placed upon it. Perhaps I would do well to remind myself of this at the remembrance and prayer meetings when I seem to have difficulty offering what I have stored up during the week.

We are not told how many guests had been invited to this supper. Bethany by the meaning of its name was associated with food, and whether at the home of Mary and Martha, or at the home of Simon the Leper, Scripture refers to hospitality freely given. During that last week it is probable that all twelve disciples, plus any women that followed along to minister to the group, were cared for here. Bethany may well have been the place to which many of the disciples fled after the arrest in Gethsemane.

In any case, a great multitude of the Jews, hearing that Jesus was there, came out of curiosity, not only to see Him, but to see Lazarus whom He had raised from the dead a short time before. Contrasted with this interest and the attention shown by those who had been with Him when Lazarus was raised and who were willing to testify to the reality of it all (v.17), were the chief priests, many of them Sadducees who did not believe in even the possibility of resurrection. The hatred of these latter was spurred on by the fact that the resurrection of Lazarus was turning many to follow Christ. Such is the power of resurrection life. Yet despicable as the official attitude was, it was superseded in heinous character by the greed of Judas.

It was not that Jesus had no care for the poor, for when Judas left the Passover feast a few days later, some thought that he had been sent to give money to the poor from the communal purse. But recognizing, as indeed Mary also must have done, that poverty would continue to characterize not only the world around, but those who would be "with you" (see Deut.15:11), and that there would be limited time to give such devotion to the Master, Christ defended her action. 'When good is prompted, evil often presents itself, but Scripture so often used this to show the beauty of that which is precious to God. So the preciousness of Mary's action stands out in great contrast to the depravity of Judas' evil. Moreover what Judas began in his carping criticism, others took up, swelling his condemnation (Mk.14:4). Murmuring is so contagious!

On the day following, the multitude from Bethany was met by the throng from Jerusalem coming to meet the One of whom they had heard. To these Jesus presented Himself as King: "Rejoice greatly, O daughter of Zion! Shout in triumph, O daughter of Jerusalem! Behold, your King is coming to you; He is just and endowed with salvation, Humble, and mounted on a donkey, Even on a colt, the foal of a donkey" (Zech.9:9). The humility of the Saviour riding upon the back of the lowly donkey was matched by His tenderness in taking along the mother of that unbroken colt, and His unwillingness to show less than due care for the animals (Mk.11:3): And immediately He will send it back here. No loss accrues to those who give for the Master's use.

The hosannas of the day would be matched by the praises of the children on the following day. We are reminded that so very often the actions of the parents are reflected in their young. In this case the children fulfilled Scripture, Psalm 8:2: "From the mouth of infants and nursing babes Thou hast established strength." When the Lord reminded those who chided Him about this scripture, those who knew their Bibles must have smarted at the context of these verses that He had quoted to them. Perhaps these shouts of those who praised were part of the antiphonal recitation of Psalm 118:25,26. Poignant indeed the context of these words also: "The stone which the builders rejected has become the chief corner stone (v.22). And "Bind the festival sacrifice with cords to the horns of the altar" (v.27).

In spite of what has been called the triumphal entry of Christ into Jerusalem, He did not come to be accepted as King. The fickle praises poured upon Him that day would soon clash with the cacophony of mob hatred. He must be rejected. And resulting from that rejection would come His own rejection of Israel. Key verses in John's gospel say this: "He came to His own, and those who were His own did not receive Him. But as many as received Him, to them gave He the right to become children of God, even to those who believe in His name (Jn.1:11.12). From the time of the praises of adults and children, there would arise discord in continuing strength until that dissonance carried the day. Yet arising out of the discord of the evil hearts of men comes a song of greater sweetness and strength, our own harmony of praise to the One who has through His rejection and death made Himself worthy to be our King:

> "Thou art my God, and I give thanks to Thee; Thou art my God, I extol Thee. Give thanks to the LORD, for He is good; For His lovingkindness is everlasting" (Ps.118:28,29).

CHAPTER ELEVEN: THESE TEN TIMES

If the ten murmurings of the children of Israel mentioned in Numbers 14:22 are all recorded in Scripture they began while Israel was still making bricks in Egypt and continued until God stood at the doors in judgement, condemning them to live and die in the wilderness, unable to enter into His rest (Heb.3:16-18).

They murmured for three reasons, the same three reasons that cause believers to murmur today: jealousy, physical hardship or the threat of it and the lack of satisfaction for physical appetites. Indeed, Israel developed such a habit of murmuring that Numbers 11:11 shows them murmuring for no apparent reason. The result was that those furthest from the tabernacle were condemned in the heat of God's anger. Physical hardship, to a greater or lesser degree, is the portion of all of us. It comes so that the grace of God can be manifested both to us and through us (Ex.15:24-27; 2 Cor.1:3-7). And it comes so that God may be glorified in us (Ex.14:11-14; Jn.9:3). Murmuring confounds the purpose of God in the hardship, adding sin and robbing us of blessing.

Physical appetites should be relegated each to its proper place and perspective. Israel wandered 38 years in the wilderness because they did not learn this. They murmured because of the bitter waters of Marah (Ex.15:24); between Elim and Sinai because of hunger (Ex.16:2); because of thirst at Rephidim (Ex.17:2). The Lord Jesus later taught the lesson they should have learned:

> "Be not therefore anxious, saying, 'What shall we eat? or, What shall we drink? or, Wherewithal shall we be clothed?' ... Your heavenly Father knoweth that ye have need of all

these things. But seek ye first His kingdom, and His righteousness; and all these things shall be added unto you" (Matt.6:31-33 RV).

"Oh, that men would praise the Lord for His goodness, and for His wonderful works to the children of men! For He satisfieth the longing soul, and the hungry soul He filleth with good" (Ps.107:8-9 RV).

The jealousy of Miriam and Aaron concerning Moses held back the progress of the whole nation, and, finally, when the people rejected the right choice of Caleb and Joshua to enter the land, arid chose to elect a captain to take them back to Egypt, God spoke in judgement: "Because all those men which have seen My glory, and My signs, which I wrought in Egypt and in the wilderness, yet have tempted Me these ten times, and have not hearkened unto My voice; surely they shall not see the land."

New Testament Scripture speaks loudly on the subject of murmuring. Paul writes: "Neither murmur ye, as some of them murmured, and perished by the destroyer. Now these things happened unto them by way of example; and they were written for our admonition, upon whom the ends of the ages are come ... God ... will not suffer you to be tempted above that ye are able" (1 Cor.10:10-13 RV).

To the Philippians (2:4 RV) he adds: "Do all things without murmurings and disputings; that ye may be blameless and harmless, children of God without blemish". James adds a solemn note (Jas.5:9 RV), "Murmur not, brethren, one against another, that ye be not judged: behold, the judge standeth before the doors".

CHAPTER TWELVE: THE DAY SHALL DECLARE IT

The apostle Paul wrote:

> "According to the grace of God which was given unto me, as a wise master-builder I laid a foundation; and another buildeth thereon. For other foundation can no man lay than that which is laid, which is Jesus Christ. But if any man buildeth on the foundation gold, silver, costly stones, wood, hay, stubble; each man's work shall be made manifest; for the day shall declare it, because it is revealed in fire; and the fire itself shall prove each man's work of what sort it is. If any man's work shall abide which he built thereon, he shall receive a reward. If any man's work shall be burned, he shall suffer loss: but he himself shall be saved; yet so as through fire (1 Cor.3:13 RV).

The festivals of the seventh month in Israel illustrate what must shortly occur in the dealings of Christ with the Church which is His body. The memorial of the blowing of trumpets on the first day is followed by a day of solemn rest on the tenth, when each Israelite must afflict his soul in self-examination before God; this in turn was to be followed by a week-long festival for which God's commandment was, "Thou shalt be altogether joyful." Leviticus 25:9,10 further associates this feast of tabernacles with the year of jubilee, a time when sowing and reaping now past gives way to an enjoyment of rich abundance from the Lord. So we also await the trumpet sound, when according to 1 Thessalonians 4:16 the dead and alive in Christ will together meet the Lord in the air to be forever with Him.

Then, before our full entry into the joy of the Lord, we must all be made manifest before the judgement seat of Christ (2 Cor.5:19). All believers will appear there, not to be examined for guilt, for that has been settled at Calvary; nor in any way to pass through fires of purification, for no such idea is taught in Scripture; but to have our works and words examined by the Son of God, to whom all judgement is given (Jn.5:22). The total conduct of every believer will come under review. Then each one of us will give oral account of himself to God (Rom.14:12). Each one will receive the things done in the body (2 Cor.5:10) and each will then have his praise from God (1 Cor.4:5).

Paul's words to the Corinthian saints in 1 Corinthians 3:10-15 also concern the judgement seat of Christ, but deal with only a part of our Christian life-that which involves building for God in a church of God upon the foundation clearly laid in Scripture.

The Church of God in Corinth is described as God's building (3:9). We believe that various churches of God, various buildings, fitly framed together form the house of God (Eph.2:21,22). Perhaps most of us have opportunity to build only locally in the Church of God to which we were added after our baptism. The foundation of such a church is no different from that of the church in Corinth laid by the apostle Paul, which is Jesus Christ. Paul laid the foundation by teaching the doctrine of Christ, the faith once for all delivered to the saints. Builders upon that foundation, then and now, will one day have their works tested by fire. It is clear, then, that the Lord is going to examine you and me who are in churches of God as to how we have dealt with the doctrine of the Lord. His impartial, all-searching fire will burn through the valueless quantity, leaving only that of quality which glorifies God and remains to the eternal credit of the builder.

It is really persons out of which the house of God is constructed, living stones built up a spiritual house (1 Pet.2:5) but it will not be individuals who are tested by the fire, some burnt, some remaining, but rather our works. We build on the foundation in the same way that Paul laid it, by adhering to the Spirit-revealed doctrine of the Lord and teaching it. His doctrine is simply what He says and which is inseparable from Himself. We live in an age when some believers would try to separate the doctrine from its Giver, when for them the very word doctrine has an unwelcome sound. In this they reflect the condition now upon us when men "will not endure the sound doctrine; but having itching ears, will heap to themselves teachers after their own lusts; and will turn away their ears from the truth ..." The Lord asked a question in Luke 6:46 (RV) that is very relevant today, "Why call ye Me Lord, Lord, and do not the things which I say? Every one that cometh unto Me, and heareth My words, and doeth them ... is like a man building his house ... upon the rock ... well builded."

What will be consumed in the fire is answerable to the thorns and thistles of Hebrews 6:8. The weedy growth of the land is there described as fit only for fire, an illustration of God's dealings with the wilful misdeeds of those who, having come to the knowledge of the truth and setting it aside, can expect only judgement and a fierceness of devouring fire upon those evil works. "The LORD shall judge His people ... and there is none that can deliver out of My hand" (Deut.32:36,39 RV; cited Heb.10:30). My behaviour in the assembly will be tempered by the remembrance that the Lord and I together will review its outcome.

How then should we build? Zechariah's fifth vision gives us a good picture: two olive branches using golden spouts to empty golden oil out of themselves into the golden lampstand. Golden oil will flow freely as we allow ourselves to be channels of the Spirit's power and leading. Paul follows his words about the judgement seat with a reminder that the Church of God is a temple of that Holy Spirit (3:16) and later that we each are a temple of that same Spirit (6:19). From His leading will develop and flow things golden, golden spoonfuls of the incense of praise overflowing from our time spent in the Word; golden ministry for the perfecting of the saints which leads to the attainment of the measure of the fulness of the stature of Christ; and golden witness, delivering those who are being carried away to death and those who are tottering to the slaughter. Apples of gold in settings of silver are all these words fitly spoken. Only in submission to the Spirit's gentle leading will the precious sons of Zion be comparable to most fine gold, vessels unto honour, sanctified, meet for the Master's use. As I pour out of myself, I build, and the church is enriched.

My building on the foundation will also affect the building of others around me. The Levitical law concerning leprosy that had broken out in the wall of a building illustrates this. When part of the wall became infected, then all that was attached to it needed to be removed also. Nathan told David that his sin had caused the enemies of the Lord to blaspheme. David on another occasion showed his appreciation of the effect that his life had on others: "Let not them that wait for Thee be ashamed through me, O Lord God of Hosts: let not those that seek Thee be brought to dishonour through me, O God of Israel" (Ps.69:6 RV).

How I build will affect my family and my dear friends. How I handle the doctrine will encourage or deter beloved saints who are also endeavouring to build to the glory of God. Some have hardship enough without my being part of their problem.

David's charge to Solomon, the builder of God's house, was: "Now set your heart and your soul to seek after the LORD your God; arise therefore, and build ye the sanctuary of the LORD God the house that is to be build to the Name of the LORD" (1 Chron.22:19 RV). Haggai echoes the thought "... build the house; and I will take pleasure in it, and I will be glorified, saith the LORD ... I am with you, saith the

LORD (Hagg.1:8,13 RV). He still is with those who build upon the foundation according to His word that in the day to come there may be to His glory and our blessing gold, silver, precious stones.

CHAPTER THIRTEEN: PERSONAL WITNESSING

Few would argue that there is a need for an effective witness for Christ in the life of every believer. In John 15:16 (RV) Jesus tells the disciples, "Ye did not choose Me, but I chose you, and appointed you, that ye should go and bear fruit ..." Paul reminds us in the epistle to the Romans that there was a time when we brought forth fruit unto death, but now we are joined to Christ who has been raised from the dead that we might bring forth fruit unto God (7:4). Soul winning is one way of bearing fruit and it is the wise one who wins souls. But it is one thing to know what we should do and quite another thing to do it and do it effectively. What are the problems that crowd in and make the best of intentions a series of regrets, and what can be done about them?

Practical Problems: Fear

Fear caused the early disciples to meet behind locked doors. Fear in many guises-fear of rejection, fear of what others might say, fear of being laughed at, fear of threat, fear of failure-causes us to retreat into the security of silence, and keeps us there even when the door of opportunity is knocked loudly. Fear is an evil emotion when it hinders the will of God. Witness is a simple, truthful telling of what the Lord has done for us. When we tell it and live it plainly no one can gainsay it. David had the answer to fear, the realization of just who was on his side: "The Lord is my light and my salvation; whom shall I fear? The Lord is the strength of my life; of whom shall I be afraid?" (Ps.27:1) "I am with you always," said Christ as He commissioned His witnesses. If God is for us, who is against us? "For God gave us not a spirit of fearfulness; but of power and love and discipline. Be not ashamed therefore of the testimony of our Lord ..." (2 Tim.1:7,8). If fear still troubles you, try sharing your concern with a praying friend. "Wait on the Lord," continued David. "Be strong, and let thy heart take courage; yea, wait thou on the Lord." Isaiah adds, "They that wait upon the Lord shall renew their strength; they shall mount up with wings as eagles; they shall run and not be weary; they shall walk, and not faint" (Is.40:31).

Comparisons

The unwise comparison of one with another caused Paul to chide the Corinthians (2 Cor.10:12), and to remind them that to do this is to lack understanding. He had previously told them that the Holy Spirit divides to each one severally even as He will. My gift, and therefore my responsibility, is not to be measured by the success of my brother or sister, or his progress in the assembly, or by his ability in personal testimony. Yet how often we are hindered because we try to match others of superior capability, and instead of imitating their faith, we are discouraged because of our lack of it. Don't be unhappy when another's ability seems to outweigh your own. Your responsibility is to the Lord, to use the talent given so that at the Master's return there will be the "well done, good and faithful servant" greeting and an entrance into the joy of the Lord. Of earthly comparisons with others Jesus said to Peter, "What is that to thee? Follow thou Me" (Jn.21:21 RV).

Pessimism

Pessimism is not a scriptural word, but it is often used by Satan as a hindrance to personal witness. "There is no point in witnessing; I would never be very good at it". "I just can't think fast enough on my feet." How often have you said it? Humility is a lovely Christian trait, but it was never meant to be a hindrance to the working of the Holy Spirit through us. What I do in my own strength is nothing (Jn.15:5). I need to remember, "It is God who worketh in you both to will and to work, for His good pleasure ... in the midst of a crooked and perverse generation, among whom ye are seen as lights in the world, holding forth the word of life" (Phil.2:13-16 RV). Pessimism is a state of mind that develops into fatalism. We each have to learn that God's power is made perfect in weakness (2 Cor.12:9), and, "I can do all things in Him that strengtheneth me" (Phil.4:13 RV).

"Busyness"

"A man turned aside and brought a man unto me, and said, 'Keep this man...' And as thy servant was busy here and there, he was gone" (1 Kin.20:39,40 RV). Does this story have any resemblance to your life? If we become collectors of earthly treasures we may fall under condemnation like Israel: "... thou servedst not the Lord thy God with joyfulness, and with gladness of heart, by reason of the abundance of all things" (Deut.28:47 RV), or like some in Philippi who minded earthly things (Phil.3:19). Busyness robs us all of opportunity to witness, yes, even busyness in assembly activity. I was once told by a salesman that he couldn't take time to serve me because he was rushing to a sales meeting. Perhaps we need the perspective that he lacked. We are all busy, for we live in a very busy world, but even the busiest will have to take time if he hopes to witness. It is all a question of priority and balance, and Martha's lesson about being concerned with many things will have to be learned by the effective witness. One day the disciples, busy with things, all visited the city of Samaria, and the town saw them come and go without ever realizing that the Lord of life and glory sat on their doorstep. One deeply-touched woman followed them into the town and led the many from there to His feet. She had things to do too, but she wasn't too busy.

Impatience

"These ... having heard the word, hold it fast, and bring forth fruit with patience" (Lk.8:15). Impatience is one of the thorns that choke the fruitbearing process. It destroyed King Saul. He just could not wait for

Samuel's arrival; just could not wait for God's acceptable time. In his impatience he lost the very kingdom he was striving for (1 Sam.13). In our witness there is a temptation to try to hurry the working of the Spirit. Like the child who tries to help the hatching chick or release the moth from its cocoon, we either destroy the thing we are trying to save or deform it so that a cripple emerges instead of a strong vital organism. Perhaps in my witness I need to read James 5:7,8 (RV) again: "Behold, the husbandman waiteth for the precious fruit of the earth, being patient over it, until it receive the early and latter rain. Be ye also patient."

Over-aggressiveness

If I have not love, I am nothing. Love suffers long, is kind, does not behave itself unseemly (see 1 Cor.13). Zeal in personal testimony is good, but there is a careful balance between zeal and over-aggressiveness. The latter spoils our witness when we press ourselves upon folk, surfeit them with attention, or turn them away with an overabundance of cloying sweetness. There is a danger of my over burdening people's minds and lives instead of waiting in prayer for the Lord to open the heart. Consider the Spirit-directed readiness of the Ethiopian eunuch's heart before Philip was called to speak to him, the necessity of Lydia's heart being opened before she could give heed to the words of Paul. We will have to wait upon the Lord for guidance to hearts already softened by the Spirit's action, and our words and actions will need to be tempered by love lest our zeal prompt an aggressiveness that might undo the gracious working of the Holy Spirit. The spirit of the hymn is good guidance: "Lead me to some soul today, and teach me Lord, just what to say."

Abiding Fruit

Here are two scriptures to consider. John 15:16 (RV): "Ye did not choose Me, but I chose you ... that ye should go and bear fruit, and that your fruit should abide." Mark 4:19 (RV): "And the cares of the world, and the deceitfulness of riches, and the lusts of other things entering in, choke the word, and it becometh unfruitful." The Lord described four categories in the parable of the sower. How can we keep those to whom we witness from falling into category three, as described by Mark? By leading them to full commitment to discipleship. The new disciple may need to be helped on the subject of eternal security and perhaps with an assurance of his salvation. He will need to be taught how to read his Bible and to pray, and should be instructed about obedience to God.

This will take additional time, perhaps many hours of it, and your own life will provide a standard for him to measure himself to, while your personal interest and continuing prayer for him will be of great encouragement as you gradually introduce him to others who are like-minded. A good Bible class or study group will greatly assist you, and appropriate reading material in moderate doses will also help. Fruitbearing is a gradual matter: first the blade, and then the ear, and then the full grain in the ear. It will only abide to bring forth fruit itself as it is tenderly nurtured through earnest prayer and loving care.

Finally, "Ye shall be my witnesses ... unto the uttermost part of the earth." We still have some ground to cover. May God help us to do so.

CHAPTER FOURTEEN: LIGHT IN THEIR DWELLINGS

The darkness that God sent as the ninth plague against Egypt was a darkness that could be felt, "so that men shall grope in darkness" (RV Margin). It answered to the spiritual state of the hearts of those who withstood the commandments of the Lord. We are now living in days of spiritual darkness in which mere men withstand the truth, even as Jannes and Jambres withstood Moses; men corrupted in mind, reprobate concerning the faith. In Egypt's darkness the children of Israel had light in their dwellings. The dwellings of God's people today should show likewise that God has put a division between all other peoples and His people. We have been delivered out of the power of darkness, translated into the kingdom of the Son of His love, having been made meet to be partakers of the inheritance of the saints in light; or as Paul told Agrippa, turned from darkness to light, and from the power of Satan unto God, having received remission of sins and an inheritance among them that are sanctified by faith in the Lord. In this world of gross darkness, the light in the dwellings of God's people should be very obvious.

Subjection

In the context of light and darkness Paul discusses subjection:

> "Ye were once darkness, but now are light in the Lord: walk as children of the light (for the fruit of the light is in all goodness and righteousness and truth) and have no fellowship with the unfruitful works of darkness ... subjecting yourselves one to another in the fear of Christ",

wives to husbands, children to parents in the Lord, servants to masters as unto Christ" (Eph.5:8-6:7 RV).

If there is light in our dwelling there will be right relationships. These in turn have their effect upon life in the assembly where brethren must also learn and show subjection (but if a man knoweth not how to rule his own house, how shall he take care of the church of God?). "Likewise, ye younger, be subject unto the elder. Yea, all of you gird yourselves with humility to serve one another" (1 Pet.5:5 RV). "He that loveth his brother abideth in the light" (1 Jn.2:10 RV). God is light, and God is love, and the two characteristics must be reflected in unfeigned love, in loving one another from the heart fervently, lest there be shadows in our dwellings where there should be light.

Truth

> "And these words which I command thee this day shall be upon thy heart; and thou shalt teach them ... in thy house ... and thou shalt write them upon the doorposts of thy house."

Deuteronomy 6:5 demands an involvement of spirit, soul and body in an active love for the Lord. The centre for teaching this was to be the home, the family circle.

> "For He established a testimony ... and appointed a law ... which He commanded our fathers, that they should make them known to their children; that the generation to come might know, even the children that should be born; who should arise and tell them to their children ..." (Ps.78:5-6 RV).

We shall make a great mistake if we leave all spiritual instruction to others, whether it be Bible class or assembly platform. Love for God and His house can be taught in the informality of the family circle, both in its activities and its conversation. We live in an age when television, books, sports, music, curricular and extracurricular academic pursuits put tremendous strain on the spirituality of the young. Godly patience and steadfastness find severe challenge in artificial drama in which all dilemma is rectified in an hour or in 300 pages, often by heroes in whom law-abiding behaviour and personal purity are sadly lacking. An affection for God's dwelling place and its present expression in churches of God seem of little consequence to the young mind whose thrill is found in sports super heroes and athletic achievement.

The Spirit of God is able counterbalance all this, of course, but there will have to be the instruction which is in righteousness based on the inspired Word of God and taught from early childhood. Not all who read this will have had that benefit, but would we also deny our children? We long for them rather, that they might be complete, furnished completely unto every good work. We live in a world of darkness where sin grows fully and brings forth death. Our light, like every other good and perfect gift, comes from the Father of lights. James links his thoughts on this with our having been brought forth by the word of truth. Without our schooling in the word of truth we will fall far short of God's standard that we should be a kind of firstfruits of His creatures.

Testimony

"The people that sat in darkness saw a great light, and to them that sat in the region and shadow of death, to them did light spring up". Where the Lord Jesus walked, light was shed abroad to others. The light of the knowledge of the glory of God in the face of Jesus Christ is a treasure we have in earthen vessels, hidden perhaps like the torches in Gideon's earthen pitchers. If so, there will need to be broken vessels, the denial of self, the arousal to the sound of trumpets and the sword of the

Lord. Your home might be the only one in your neighborhood where there is light, a veritable potential lighthouse in a sea of men groping in darkness. We can hide our light under the bushel of business or under the bed of sloth, but the command is to let our light so shine before men that they may see our good works and glorify our Father who is in heaven. The believer's home is an ideal place for such witness.

In the city of Victoria, B.C., there are two important buildings a short distance from one another. The Parliament buildings are a picture of lights, an evening attraction to tourists, a delightful display. The nearby harbour lighthouse has just one light, set and timed for the safety of those around. Does my house have its light only to shine on itself for its own beauty when men die in darkness at our sides without a hope?

Hospitality

What a light to weary Elisha must have been the house of the woman of Shunem! In an increasing intensity of gloom what a light to the Saviour must have been the humble abode of Mary and Martha in Bethany! Dear Lydia and her house of light were a light to Paul, and to the Spirit of God who caused these words to be recorded: "If ye have judged me to be faithful to the Lord, come into my house and abide there. And she constrained us". God requires of men given to the leadership of His people that they be hospitable (1 Tim.3:2). Hospitality is further commanded to all the saints in Romans 12:13. Peter says, "But the end of all things is at hand: be fervent in your love among yourselves ... using hospitality one to another without murmuring". Hebrews 13:2 extends it a little further: "Forget not to show love unto strangers: for thereby some have entertained angels unawares". And the King shall answer and say unto them, "Verily I say unto you, Inasmuch as ye did it unto one of these My brethren, even these least, ye did it unto Me."

"There was a thick darkness in all the land of Egypt ... They saw not one another, neither rose any from his place ... but all the children of

Israel had light in their dwellings". God was later to put a thick and intense darkness between Egypt and Israel. Egypt went from darkness to darkness, but Israel marched in light (Ex.14:20 RV). "The way of the wicked is as darkness: they know not at what they stumble" (Prov.4:19 RV). "But the path of the righteous is as the shining light, that shineth more and more unto the perfect day" (v.18 RV).

CHAPTER FIFTEEN: THE SIN OFFERINGS

Sin blinds the eyes, fouls the conscience, and separates between man and God. With its close relatives, iniquity and transgression, it has its origin in Satan, runs rampant through the total depravity of man, and comprises anything and everything that is contrary to the character of God.

The Lord Jesus Christ in His one sacrifice for sins for ever made purification of sins, put away sin by the sacrifice of Himself, and enabled God never more to remember the sins and lawlessness of His New Covenant people. Until the sacrifice of Christ at Calvary, sin was covered over through the various offerings appropriated and offered for the purpose according to the will of God. These sin offerings and the great Sin Offering of whom they speak are the subject of this chapter.

It must be remembered that the Levitical offerings were commanded for a people already redeemed, and were compulsory if fellowship with God was to be maintained. These were ordained for individuals who might sin in coming short of God's standard (Lev.4); or who incurred guilt through certain specific unwitting offences (Lev.5:1-13); or unintentional faithlessness in the types of trespasses that caused loss and demanded restitution as well as sacrifice (Lev.5:14-6:7). They were also compulsory for the sin and trespass of God's people. Both then and today a collective people might sin. The nation might fall into idolatry, rulers might lead them astray, teachers through sinning themselves might cause the people to sin. Wherever, whenever, and however sin is committed, sin is sin, and must be dealt with that there might be reconciliation with God: "He made Him ... to be sin on our behalf, that we might become the righteousness of God in Him" (2 Cor.5:21).

The value of the sacrifice varied according to the position of knowledge and responsibility of the one sinning: high position - high responsibility. The sin of a priest was equal to the sin of the whole people and required a bullock; a ruler needed a male goat; and the common people were to offer a female kid or lamb. In every case there was identification with the offering. In the case of the people, the elders acted by placing their hands on the head of the bullock involved.

On behalf of the people or a priest the blood was apportioned according to the area of service in the house that was affected by the sin. For the nation or priest - before the Lord, before the veil, on the altar of incense and at the base of the copper altar. For the ruler or one of the people, the blood remained outside the holies, on the horns of the copper altar and at its base. The blood that went in was applied on the way out and not on the way in. Expiation was from God, not man.

The study of the application of blood, wider than the parameters of this article, is an important inquiry. The blood of Christ has also done what the blood of animals could never do in that it took away sins (Heb.10:4). However, the blood of these animals does teach us about the effects of His sacrifice. The teaching differs according to the place and way in which the blood was applied.

The blood of the passover spoke redemption for the people of God (Ex.12:23). In the wilderness in front of Sinai, it sealed the covenant (Ex.24:8), and in the Levitical offerings and especially on the day of atonement it atoned for sin (Lev.17:11). The blood of Christ, of which the blood of these offerings was a shadow, effects justification (Rom.5:9), procures redemption (Eph.1:7), reconciles to God (Col.1:20), brings the believer near to God (Eph.2:13), and cleanses from all sins (1 Jn.1:7). On behalf of the collective people of God it was essential for the ratification of the new covenant (1 Cor.11:25), loosing from sins and redeeming this collective entity to constitute it a holy nation, a kingdom, and priests unto His God and Father (1 Pet.1:18,19; Rev.1:5,6). It is His blood too which purges the conscience for collective service (Heb.9:14), and has inaugurated the new and living access whereby we may enter the holies (Heb.10:19).

In the cases of both individual and national sin the sweetness of the fat was placed on the altar of burnt offering, just as the appropriate parts of the burnt and peace offerings had been. Though the various sin offerings could not usually be seen as sweet savour offerings of Christ, there was something exceedingly precious to God in Christ's offering of Himself without blemish unto Him. Only God could fully appreciate it.

In the offering for the people, the carcass was borne outside the camp to be consumed by fire. Hebrews 13:11-13 clarifies the teaching of this for us in a very practical way. The body was removed from the presence of God to meet man's need in respect to the judgement of his sin. The blood was taken into the presence of God to meet God's demands for man's reconciliation.

In the event of an individual's sacrifice, after the blood had been applied and God has had His portion, the balance of the sheep or goat was eaten by the priest, for the labourer is worthy of his hire, and the priesthood, affected by the sin of others must also rejoice in its forgiveness. Nevertheless, the priest must then scour and rinse the brazen pot or break the earthenware vessel that had touched the offering. The offerer received nothing of the sacrifice. The grace of God had again triumphed through the death of the innocent. Sin had been forgiven. It is noteworthy that on the day of atonement, the confession of the sins of the people over the head of the living goat was made after the slaughter of the goat of the sin offering for the people. The holies had meantime been cleansed by blood, so that the services of the people of God might flow to Him (Lev.16:15,21).

The uses of the four sides of the copper altar also speak lessons to us worthy of further study. On the north side the burnt offering was slain, showing our acceptance before God (Lev.1:11). On the east side, the ashes were deposited, perhaps portraying our justification (Lev.1:16). On the west side the peace offering was slain, speaking of our access and fellowship (Lev.3:2). And on the south side His future kingdom will flow that river of cleansing and sanctification for the whole world (Ezek.47:1).

Through the laying on of hands, then, the sin had been laid upon the offering. Through the application of the blood, the righteousness of the offering was imputed to the offerer. Through the cleansing of the holies there was a place for divine service by the people of God, which we also enjoy on the first day of the week in the very presence of Christ and of God.

The Trespass Offering

Trespass grew out of unwitting carelessness: concealing the truth (Lev.5:1), defilement through association (vv.2,3), not keeping one's promises (v.4) or unintentional dishonesty Godward or manward (v.15).

There was and is no sacrifice for intentional, wilful sin (Heb.10:26), but even though the matter was unintentional and for a time unrecognized, it was trespass, and when it was known it required sacrifice. There is in this a solemn reminder to all of us that sin renders us unfit for divine service. Failure to return borrowed goods, unfairness in fellowship, coercion, deception and false pretences, and the keeping of things found constitute trespass, even when the action is in no way deliberate.

Robbing man required sacrifice to God because it was a sin against Him also, and it required restitution to the person robbed. Robbing God (Mal.3:8) demanded sacrifice, and the priest's estimation of damages and restitution to Him. To both God and man the offender must add a fifth part. In both cases there was to be confession of the particular sin involved. Forgiveness by God was guaranteed, and forgiveness by man was demanded where one was involved. If the sin was manward, the offering to God was a female kid or lamb, or two turtledoves or young pigeons, or the tenth part of an ephah of fine flour, according to the financial ability of the offerer. Where the sin was against God only, there must be offered a ram without defect, whether or not the offerer felt he could afford it.

In all cases of animal offering for trespass, the fat, kidneys and covering of the liver went to the altar for God. The priest who made atonement acquired all the rest. The offerer retained nothing. In the case of specific guilt of the very poor the second bird or a handful of flour went to the altar. The priest received the rest of the flour.

Adam's Trespass

In the trespass of Adam both God and man were robbed. Who can contemplate the tremendous payment that must be made to compensate? Isaiah 53 floods our hearts with appreciation: He was cut off out of the land of the living, for the transgression of my people to whom the stroke was due. The total claims of God and full restitution to man were achieved in the offering of Christ: God was in Christ reconciling the world to Himself, not counting their trespasses against them (2 Cor.5:19).

And: "When you were dead in your transgressions ... He made you alive together with Him, having forgiven us all our transgressions, having cancelled out the ... debt ... and He has taken It out of the way, having nailed it to the cross" (Col.2:13,14). And: "For if by the transgression of the one the many died, much more did the grace of God and the gift by the grace of the one Man, Jesus Christ, abound to the many" (Rom.5:15).

God lost through Adam's transgression. But He has received full recompense and more through the sacrifice of Christ, the giver of the "fifth part". Man has lost through the transgression of Adam. But by one offering, the Lord Jesus Christ has procured full restitution and the "fifth part" - more than we in Adam ever lost. Blessed, holy, spotless sacrifice, the complete fulfilment of all God's purposes in Him, and the One through whom we have all our forgiveness, acceptance, peace and fellowship, yes, and all things.

For: "He who did not spare His own Son, but delivered Him up for us all, how will He not also with Him freely give us all things?" (Rom.8:32). Sin which blinded, fouled and separated has been done away through His one offering. Thanks be to God for His indescribable gift!

CHAPTER SIXTEEN: THE SWEET SAVOUR OFFERINGS

The tabernacle and its services are a parable for today (Heb.9:9), a time in which God is also, as in Moses' day, related to a people through covenant. The importance of Leviticus is indicated by the numerous New Testament references. Crucial to Israel's walk and our own is an understanding of God's purpose in sacrifice.

The burnt offering, meal offering, and peace offering are those which sent forth a soothing aroma from the altar to God. In them are typified the merit and perfection of the Lord Jesus Christ and also our acceptance and fellowship through Him. In the sin and trespass offerings, the sinful demerit and imperfection of mankind as borne by the Saviour are pictured, and our forgiveness through Him. These were not sweet savour offerings. No single offering could ever give expression to all the blessings of divine grace that would flow from the one great and complete sacrifice of the Lord Jesus Christ at Calvary.

The Burnt Offering

Various animals were offered according to the wealth and ability of the offerer. The burnt offering was presented not only for an individual whose heart overflowed in appreciation of his acceptance before the Lord, but also for a collective people. This was voluntary for the individual, but compulsory for the people on a daily basis. The rules for the burnt offering changed when it was presented in connection with some of the seven festivals of the Lord. Some of the sweetest lessons come from meditation on those changes.

The individual could offer a bullock, sheep, goat, dove or pigeon. A qualifying criterion was the ability of the offerer to give. How could an offerer then or now, if he had an appreciation of his acceptability before God, give beneath his ability? Paul says: "if the readiness is present, it is acceptable according to what a man has, not according to what he does not have ... God loves a cheerful giver" (2 Cor.8:12; 9:7). But woe to him who robs God by giving less than he is able! (See Mal.1:8; 3:8). "How much do you owe to my master?" though used in a different context is still a pertinent question (Lk.16:5).

The offerer brought his sacrifice to the door of the tabernacle, for God's house was to be the only place of such devotion. He must then identify himself with the animal, thereby acknowledging that his acceptability was not in himself, but in the perfection of the sacrifice. The carcass, properly divided, revealed purity in every part, and whether it was the head, the seat of intellect; or the inwards, the will and affections; or the legs, the outward walk and conduct; all spoke of the One of whom it is said:

He knew no sin (2 Cor.5:21).

In Him there is no sin (1 Jn.3:5).

(He) committed no sin (1 Pet.2:22).

(He was) without sin (Heb.4:15).

All was offered without any part being reserved for the offerer. The priest for his labour received the hide. All else went to the altar. In our appreciation of the Lord as our burnt offering, we need also pay attention to Paul's word to the Romans: "Present your bodies a living and holy sacrifice, acceptable to God, which is your spiritual service" (Rom.12:1). This will cause us to: "walk in love, just as Christ also loved you and gave Himself up for us, an offering and a sacrifice to God as a fragrant aroma" (Eph.5:2). And it will affect our works also: "How much more will the blood of Christ, who through the eternal Spirit offered Himself without blemish to God, cleanse your conscience from dead works to serve the living God?" (Heb.9:14).

Israel's daily compulsory offering assured the continuing acceptance of the people on the basis of sacrifice. It reminded them that only on that basis could they continue, a matter that will be still remembered by Israel in the millennial kingdom. The variations or changes of rules in offering for the national festivals included the doubling of the offering on the sabbath. Entering into the rest of God then or now requires an enhanced appreciation of the burnt offering aspect of Christ. This touches His own acceptability before God and ours through Him. The greatly extended offering on the first day of each month was a continual marking of the grace of God as He accepted His people on the basis of sacrifice.

The Meal Offering

The Hebrew word for meal offering is 'minchah' and indicates the gift of a person to his superior. It took the form of fine wheaten flour, cakes, or roasted grains, with salt, and to some were added oil and incense. Generally, a handful was placed on the altar; the balance was for the priest, "a thing most holy". All the incense was offered on the altar, the sweetness of the incense from the golden altar and the sweetness from the altar of burnt offering ascending together. The burnt and peace offerings were always accompanied by a meal offering, its size depending on the size of the sacrifice, though it could also be offered in other ways (see Lev.23:16; Num.5:15).

Even taking a cautious view of typology there is in the meal offering room for meditation on the incense that went to the altar, God alone fully appreciating the fulness of the sweetness of Christ. We may also meditate on. that upon which the priest fed, or upon the grinding, roasting, mixing with oil and salt, and parching before the fire or other cooking methods, all representative of the marvellous aspects of the life of the Lord Jesus Christ on earth and in resurrection also.

Variations

When the meal offering was for a poor man's guilt (Lev.5:11-13), or for the sin of jealousy (Num.5:15), there was neither oil nor frankincense added. Sin and guilt are not the result of the Spirit's work. In Leviticus 7:11-13 the Offering of meal consists of leavened and unleavened cakes together. In the work of the priesthood there will need to be some resemblance between the life of the offerer and the life of the offering, as both are presented together. On the beginning of each month the meal offering was increased in association with the increase in the burnt offering, perhaps a continuing reminder of the character of life that God sought among His people. And when the sheaf of firstfruits was offered on that day which was later to become the resurrection day, which it also typified, the meal offering with the he-lamb of the burnt offering was doubled; for resurrection life and our blessings through it were the major considerations (Lev.23:13). The new wave offering of the feast of weeks included two loaves on the wave breast which were of this same double size, reminding us that God had from Pentecost a nation whose life was important

One "Producing the Fruit (Of the Kingdom)"

On special occasions when the Israelites enjoyed the firstfruits of the land or the firstfruits of the threshing floor, meal was to be heaved up as thanksgiving to the Lord, just as we also offer from overflowing hearts when we read and meditate on the blessings of the land or the lessons of the threshing floor (Ruth 3; 1 Chron.21:22). To be unintentionally thankless at such times demanded a sin offering. The meal offerings were of great importance to Israel, and the life of Christ which they suggest to us is similarly of tremendous value.

The Peace Offering

The third sweet savour offering (Lev.3) was to be divided among God, the priest and the offerer, and to all it was exceedingly sweet. In the peace offering, friendship and fellowship were celebrated in a linked appreciation of the goodness of God. No birds were allowed here; the celebration of fellowship demands a spiritual wealth which could not be characterized by less than a sheep, goat, or bullock. That either gender might be used enhances the concept of fellowship seen in the offering. God's portion of this offering must be presented on the altar first the outer and inner fat, the kidneys or reins and the caul upon the liver. Meditation on each brings a wealth of thought as it is applied to what God the Father received from His Son's sacrifice. That these were always offered on the altar upon the burnt offering shows the close link between our acceptance in Christ and the peace and fellowship which should follow.

The priest received the wave breast and the heave thigh. His whole family might enjoy this with him. So those who as a priesthood serve God today share in a feasting on the affection and strength that these special parts represent. In this fellowship offering all the rest of the animal was for the offerer and his family. Fellowship grows in quality the more we understand God's appreciation of the sacrifice of Christ. "We have peace with God through our Lord Jesus Christ" (Rom.5:1). "(He) made peace through the blood of His cross" (Col.1:20). "He Himself is our peace" (Eph.2:14).

Some imperfect animals might also be offered, because of poverty, as fellowship offerings of thanksgiving (Lev.22:21-25), but this in no way indicated imperfection in the One who is the fulfilment of all such sacrifices. Rather, it indicates God's acceptance of thanksgiving even though there is imperfection in the appreciation of the offerer.

The peace offering of the feast of weeks is a pre-figuring of Pentecost and the beginning of that new movement of which we are a part who serve God in His house today. There is a special affectionate relationship between loaves and wave breast, even as there is between Christ and God's people. The offerings of Leviticus were peculiar to a called-out and called-together nation, and were to be sacrificed and eaten in the place of the Name (Deut. 12:27). These provide a rewarding study and meditation as we contemplate the special revelation of the Lord Jesus Christ seen in them, and His association with those who are found in God's house today.

CHAPTER SEVENTEEN: THE SHEPHERD'S RODS

There was more than good animal husbandry in the breeding of the sheep and goats under Jacob's care. God gave the herds of Laban to Jacob (Gen.31:10), and we marvel at the miracle that overrode Laban's lack of fidelity to Jacob. There is a word in all this for shepherds today who would feed the flock which He purchased with the blood of His own One. The character of the flock is determined by the character of the rod held in front of it when it comes to the watering-troughs. Micah (7:14) warned Israel's shepherds: "Feed thy people with thy rod, the flock of thine heritage ... let them feed ... as in the days of old". And Ezekiel's scathing condemnation of shepherds in his day shows the seriousness of failing to care for and feed the flock of God (Ezek.34). "Should not the shepherds feed the sheep? ... but ye feed not the sheep. And they were scattered, because there was no shepherd: and they became meat to all the beasts of the field ... My sheep were scattered ... and there was none that did search or seek alter them" (vv.2-6). The character of the flock again was determined by the shepherds.

The Proverb wisely exhorts: "Be thou diligent to know the state of thy flocks, and look well to thy herds" (27:23). Paul told the shepherds of Ephesus a similar message. Men would arise from among them who would speak perverse things and draw away the disciples. Shepherds on the other hand who feed the flock with knowledge and understanding are shepherds after God's own heart (Jer.3:15). All shepherds will soon enough have to answer the question, "Where is the flock that was given to thee, thy beautiful flock?" (Jer.13:20; Heb.13:17). The promise of showers of blessing, about which we sing and for which we long, depends upon proper shepherd care and proper feeding (Ezek.34:26).

While responsibility for shepherd care and proper feeding begins with the leaders, the sheep also have their responsibilities. "Hear ye the rod and who hath appointed it" (Mic.6:9). Zechariah gives many lessons to both (chapter 11). Whatever the flock's condition, beauty and bands must be the character of the rods lifted before them. The beauty of the Lord must be the appeal of the food presented, and that which binds together in unity its effect. But the ultimate responsibility to receive and ingest this belongs to the flock, as Zechariah 11 clearly indicates. In their rejection of the beauty and unity held on the staves before them, Israel lost the opportunity to be found in the character of the One that they rejected, and were in turn rejected by Him. We who have returned to the Shepherd and Bishop of our souls need to take upon us His character; He left us an example that we should follow His steps. How great is His goodness, and how great is His beauty!

In the vision of the valley of dry bones Ezekiel saw bones coming together according to the word of Jehovah, bone to its bone. Accompanying this vision came the illustration of the two rods:

> "Take thee one stick, and write upon it, for Judah, and for the children of Israel his companions: then take another stick and write upon it, for Joseph, the stick of Ephraim, and for all the house of Israel his companions: and join them into one stick, that they may become one in thine hand ... I ... will gather them ... and I will make of them one nation in the land" (Ezek.37:16-22).

That the children of God today should be gathered into one was the John 17 prayer of the Lord Jesus. Undershepherds, ensamples to the flock, will need to give consistent heed to 1 Peter 5 which deals with the matter. Subjection, humility and service one to another will be the basis of the unity projected, a reflection of the underlying love that keeps us together. And where there is anxiety, there will be the need to cast it upon Him who careth for us. Only in this way will bone and bone, stick and stick become and maintain a unity. Only in the unity of elderhood will there be unity of flock.

CHAPTER EIGHTEEN: PROPHETS OF REVIVAL!

Revival! Godly men in darkened days have always longed for it! The cry of Habakkuk in a time of impending judgement was: "O Lord, revive Thy work in the midst of the years, in the midst of the years make it known" (Hab.3:2 RV). Ezra acknowledged the grace of God in bringing from captivity a remnant with a nail in His holy place ... reviving to setup the house of God (Ezra 9:8,9). Revival is stones from the rubble (Neh.4:2); it is the bringing forth of grain and wine after the unfruitfulness of winter (Hos.14:7); it is the lifting of the humble spirit and the contrite heart (Is.57:15). Our own souls long for it.

Yet adversaries without, apathy among many believers, and an unsympathetic environment all diminish its probability. In days much like our own, God reminded the people through two prophets, Haggai and Zechariah, that He was the One able to shake heavens and earth and to pour down blessing upon His people.

The year was 520 B.C. Fourteen years previously under Zerubbabel's direction the foundation of the house of God had been laid. Then Cyrus of Persia died in 529 B.C. and an unsympathetic Ahasuerus came to power and lent an ear to Samaritan counsellors who convinced him that work on the temple should be suspended. In 520 B.C., what should have been a glorious house lay waste, overgrown with weeds and scarred by debris. Crop failure and economic recession caused the people to consolidate their financial position to secure personal comfort, but this brought neither contentment nor divine approbation. Lack of blessing both temporal and spiritual was accepted with gloomy resignation. In the midst of this, God gave four clear messages through Haggai in a period of four months and supplemented those with a series of visions and promises through his contemporary, Zechariah, all to the same intent: build the house; I am with you; I will bless you. Haggai's two chapters are delightfully simple and straightforward; Zechariah's fourteen are far-reaching and complex, but both contain a message for Israel and for our own age about the subject of revival (Rom.15:4).

The command of God had not changed: "Whosoever there is among you of all His people, his God by with him, and let him go up to Jerusalem which is in Judah, and build the house of the Lord" (Ezra 1:3); nor had any the authority to change that word no matter what the circumstance. The commandment was the more important because of the soon coming of the Lord Jesus Christ, to which Haggai alludes in 2:7,9, "the desire (KJV) of all nations shall come ... the latter glory of this house shall be greater than the former" ... (While arguments have surrounded these verses as to whether Messiah's coming to His temple is meant, all things considered I read the verses in that way).

This commandment to build is a reflection of the commission of the Lord Jesus to His disciples in Matthew 28:19. "Go ye therefore" was Haggai's message, and the Lord's. And once again the blessed pope, even the appearing of our great God and Saviour Jesus Christ lends urgency to our obedience. Unfortunately, a "day of small things" led the people to say that it was not the right time to build the house. Haggai's four-fold message instructs all, whether hampered by prevailing philosophy or misinterpretation of Scripture. The house is to be built.

The first communication invites Israel to a consideration of their present state, an evaluation of living without due thought to divine commandment, the result of which is always much labour, little benefit. The second pleads with the people to realize that God is with them, and is reminiscent of that later, "Lo, I am with you alway". God was with them by covenant (2:5); His Spirit abode among them and His promise remained sure, reiterated for our own benefit in Hebrews 12:26,27 (RV):

> "... now He hath promised, saying, Yet once more will I make to tremble not the earth only, but also the heaven. And this word, yet once more, signifieth the removing of those things that are shaken, as of things that have been made, that those things that are not shaken may remain. Wherefore receiving a kingdom that cannot be shaken, let us have thankfulness (RV margin), whereby we may offer service well-pleasing unto God with reverence and awe: for our God is a consuming fire".

Haggai's third message reminds us that mere working on a holy project does not in itself make one holy. Association with dead works always renders one unclean. Thank God for repentance from dead works and the blood of Christ which cleanses the conscience from dead works, that in our day we may serve the living God. Our engagement in the building of God's house puts God under no obligation to bless. It is in His abounding grace that He deigns to use the efforts of men and to give the promise of any present or future blessing. Haggai's fourth message is directly to Zerubbabel, yet shows us in him God's greater Leader. Zerubbabel was to be God's signet, His sign of authority in that day; in the present and in days shortly to unfold will the signet of God be impressed upon men through His greater Leader, for He is yet to be glorified in His saints and marvelled at in them that behaved (2 Thess.1:10).

Between Haggai's second and third messages, Zechariah began to amplify what Haggai had been saying, particularly in Zechariah 1 to 8. In the following chapters we are taken far beyond temple-building days of the past to future ultimate triumph in Israel under Christ, when all to do with Israel will be holy unto Jehovah. It would seem that the visions of the first eight chapters of Zechariah came all in one night (Zech.1:7), just five months after the rebuilding of the temple had been resumed. The first shows the divinely ordained interest of heavenly beings in earthly things, especially in things to do with the building of the house of God. Hebrews 1:14 tells us that this same interest obtains today.

The second and third visions promise divine intervention in the nations so that God's purposes might be carried out and His servants protected, a matter which finds concurrence both in relation to the words of Moses in Deuteronomy 32:8 for Israel in the past, and to Paul's in 1 Corinthians 3:16,17 for God's people in this age. The calling out and together of a people and the furnishing of that people for the fulfilment of divine service is ever a priority item with God. Joshua, high priest over a covenanted people is to be reclothed in vision four, and the Old Covenant still in effect, renewed through the cleansing of people and priesthood, but points forward to the new one under which we now serve.

Christ is a priest of good things now come, through the greater and more perfect tabernacle (Heb.9:11), and God's people are seen together in sanctification of the Spirit, unto obedience and the sprinkling of the blood of Jesus Christ (1 Pet.1:2). Notice for interest the nine times in the book of Hebrews where the Lord is called Jesus, the same name as Joshua, this Old Covenant high priest.

Vision five shows an earth-based witness (compare Revelation 1:20) into which fruit-bearing branches, "sons of oil", become channels which receive from the Lord beside whom they stand and pour forth that which is received to the sustaining and brightening of the testimony. Whatever all the explanations of the sixth vision of scroll and ephah might be, one thing is very clear. What is described by the angel as wickedness and associated with the curse has no place in the house of God. Wickedness pertains to Babylon and must be delivered there. Vision seven again emphasizes the working of the great powers in heaven in the fulfilling of divine purpose upon the earth; shows the triumphant crowning of Joshua the high priest, reflecting the victory of the Lord in the re-establishing of His people; and finally points forward to the Branch, who in a yet future day will build the temple of Jehovah.

The visions given to Zechariah by an unchanging God along with the four messages through Haggai should speak great encouragement to God's people who long for revival in our day. We must consider our ways; cleanse ourselves from all defilement of flesh and spirit, perfecting holiness in the fear of God (2 Cor.7:1); and build the house, ever aware of God's interest, presence and power with us. Words such as, "I am with you", "he that toucheth you toucheth the apple of His eye", "I will take pleasure in it (the house), and I will be glorified, saith the LORD", should urge us on to a fulfilment of His purposes in us. God "willeth that all men should be saved, and come to the knowledge of the truth" (1 Tim.2:4 RV).

CHAPTER NINETEEN: JEALOUSY

Jealousy steals the peace of God from the heart. It moved the ten patriarchs against Joseph their brother, and they sold him into Egypt. It prompted Eliab, the elder brother of David, to chide him for leaving his sheep, to rescue Israel from the hand of Goliath and the Philistines. It tempted Saul to despise David and to hunt him like a partridge upon the mountains. Jealousy was that which caused the high priest and Sadducees to jail the apostles. It is cruel as Sheol, its flashes as flashes of fire, a most vehement flame. It is linked with strife, the lusts of the flesh and all the works of darkness: the antithesis of all that is involved in putting on the Lord Jesus Christ (Rom.13:12-14).

All the works of the flesh that stand against the fruit of the Spirit and bar full entrance into the kingdom of God (Gal.5:19-24) are connected with it. "Where jealousy and faction are, there is confusion and every vile deed" (Jas.3:16). Jealousy eats like a cancer, feeding its own appetite with an even greater one, growing out of and again into vainglory, provocation and envy, robbing from us the joy of walking with the Spirit and enjoying the precious things He has for us. Jealousy in its extreme has wrecked lives, families, assemblies. But even in its initial stages it robs the Lord of the quality of offering we place in His hands Lord's day by Lord's day as we function as a holy priesthood, offering up spiritual sacrifices acceptable to God through Jesus Christ. What is the remedy?

Philippians 4 deals with the remedy of all problems involving interpersonal relationships. Rejoice in the Lord. In nothing be anxious. Whatsoever things are honourable, just, pure, lovely, of good report, things of virtue, things praiseworthy, take account of these things. It is surprising how jealousy drops away as we learn that we can do all things through the One who strengthens us. Jealousy grows out of a combination of inadequacy and pride, but when we commit ourselves and our feelings to the Lord and leave them with Him, they are crucified: we walk away from the cross and leave them there (Gal.5:24).

> "Put on therefore, as God's elect, holy and beloved, a heart of compassion, kindness, humility, meekness, longsuffering; forbearing one another, and forgiving each other ... put on love ... And let the peace of Christ rule in your hearts" (Col.3:12-15).

CHAPTER TWENTY: THE QUIET TIME

Most readers will not need to be convinced that a daily time alone with God is vital for successful Christian living. But it is one thing to know this, another to use it, and still another to use it to best advantage. A more dedicated application of ourselves to this daily devotional period may be the necessary ingredient for greater victory in both our individual and collective living. This article shares a few thoughts about establishing a time and using it wisely.

You live in a world that is no friend to the One you serve. Nor will this world feed you with the food necessary for you to thrive on your heavenly journey. Your walk demands fellowship with God, a communion of your heart with His, a quiet listening to His tender voice. So, the need for the Quiet Time. Use the Lord Jesus as your example:

> "The Lord GOD hath given Me the tongue of them that are taught, that I should know how to sustain with words him that is weary: He wakeneth morning by morning, He wakeneth Mine ear to hear ..." (Is.50:4 RV).

"Them that honour Me," says He, "I will honour." Morning, before the clutter of the day encroaches on us, may be the best time, but whether then or another time, do fix a time when you can be unhurried and alone. Prayerfully commit this time to God and then consider it the most important of all daily appointments. Find a quiet place where you can pursue your devotions without interruption. You will need a few moments to begin with to quieten your spirit and to develop a sense of expectancy, to discipline your mind, and to avoid preoccupation with self. Expect to delight yourself in the Lord. Expect to pray and have your prayers answered, and expect to receive a gem from the Word of God. This will not be done in a spirit of hurry or worry. Do not use this devotional time to prepare for meeting or Sunday School. Quiet Time is not for task preparation or education; it is for feasting upon the Lord. Prepare your heart for it. Do not hurry through it. The busier you are, the more you need it (Eccl.9:10).

Begin your time in prayer. Not just a reciting of things that you need, but a confession of your sins, your weaknesses, your problems. Purge yourself of these things. Then give yourself to thanksgiving, not only for things, but for Christ and all that He means to you. Next there will be others and their problems to lay before the Lord. Then your own needs may occupy your prayer. When Job prayed for his friends, God turned his captivity and began to give him more than he had ever had before.

Bible reading is next. Read according to a plan - not too much at any one time - maybe a dozen verses or a short chapter, but read it through two or three times to help it settle in your mind and heart. Use the Scriptures alone in your quiet time. Meditate on the word itself. Commentaries and helps have their place, but at some other time. Jot down short notes, a recall help for other times, perhaps including from your portion one sin to be forsaken, a promise to be claimed, a special revelation of some facet of the character of Christ, an example to be followed, a commandment to be obeyed, or a pitfall to be avoided. Ask yourself just what this reading can do for you today, and then see how the Spirit of God brings it to mind in the busy hours that follow.

There are a few additional practical aids which you might find helpful. Do all in your power to preserve the time without interruption. Don't do all the talking - listen. Don't try to crowd in too much reading. Do give yourself at least twenty minutes, and more if possible, but quality is better than quantity. If you have to miss a day, don't feel that the whole day is wasted. Confess your failure to keep the appointment, and get back on track as soon as possible. Don't skip the Lord's Day, even though you will be spending much of it in spiritual pursuits. Work for the Lord does not replace sitting at His feet, as we need to learn, as did Martha.

Finally, commit your day to the Lord, to guide you through it and to use it and to use you to glorify Himself. It will not be long before you begin to reap the harvest of your Quiet Time. And this is a reaping the results of which will go on throughout eternity.

"Take time to be holy, the world rushes on;

Spend much time in secret with Jesus alone.

By looking to Jesus, like Him thou shalt be;

Thy friends in thy conduct His likeness shall see.

Take time to be holy, let Him be thy Guide;

And run not before Him, whatever betide;

In joy or in sorrow still follow thy Lord,

And looking to Jesus, still trust in His word.

Take time to be holy, be calm in thy soul,

Each thought and each temper beneath His control.

Thus led by His Spirit and filled with His love

Thou soon shalt be fitted for service above".

CHAPTER TWENTY-ONE: FURNISHED LIBERALLY

In the seventh year the Hebrew servant, if he should take his liberty, must be freed and furnished liberally in his new freedom. "Thou shalt furnish him liberally out of thy flock, and out of thy threshing-floor, and out of thy wine press: as the LORD thy God hath blessed thee thou shalt give unto him" (Deut.15:14 RV). In doing this the liberator was to remember that he had been a bondman in Egypt, and he might well remember too that he had been furnished liberally in the Exodus with materials that he might bring to his God as a freewill offering (Ex.12:35,6; 35:5-9).

"And we have known redemption, Lord,

From bondage worse than theirs by far;

Sin held us by a stronger cord,

Yet by Thy mercy free we are."

In our freedom we too have been furnished liberally. The blessings accompanying freedom were a reflection of divine blessing. What about our own blessings? We have Christ, the precious Lamb of God, and in Him every spiritual blessing in the heavenlies. "He that spared not His own Son, but delivered Him up for us all, how shall He not also with Him freely give us all things?" Of Israel, Asaph wrote: "He should feed them also with the finest of the wheat: and with honey out of the rock should I satisfy thee". Yet in all their feeding and feasting they were never fed as we have been. "My Father giveth you the true bread out of heaven. For the bread of God is that which cometh down out of heaven, and giveth life unto the world ... Jesus said unto them,

I am the bread of life: he that cometh to Me shall not hunger". Asaph knew all about the threshing-floor, for the house of God was built upon a threshing-floor in Solomon's day. So is the place of His Name today.

In the house of God the Israelite was given the opportunity to give to God again of that which he had been given. Scripture records the happy results of opportunity well taken: "So the people were restrained from bringing. For the stuff they had was sufficient for all the work to make it, and too much" (Ex.36:6-7). Can we who have been freed and so liberally furnished do less than bring to God again?

Why should I keep one precious thing from Thee,

When Thou hast given Thine own dear self for me?

CHAPTER TWENTY-TWO: A CHOSEN RACE

God is a God of sovereign choices (1), many of which select the few from very many. From the vastness of space and an innumerable array of galaxies in the universe, all of His creation, God chose the one in which we live. It is so large in its rotation around its centre that it is estimated that it would take the sun 225 million years to make a complete circuit. Our galaxy is 100,000 light years in diameter; and from its profusion of heavenly bodies God chose this planet, so tiny in the diversity and scheme of space.

'Tis on earth the Lord discloses

All His love how vast it is;

Earth's the favoured spot He chooses

To display the truth of this

That God is love. (T. Kelly)

He then chose humanity out of the myriad of living species of this creation (2), and from those that issued from the first Adam He chose the godly line of Seth, through the godly line of Shem, then the godly line of Abraham (3), from whom were born various races. One in particular was God's choice: Israel. Of the vast number of races upon the earth, whom Isaiah describes as 'a drop in a bucket', a speck of 'dust on the scales' (4), God loved Israel because He loved them (5), made a choice, and called them, "Israel whom I have chosen" (6) - not because they were anything, but when they were nothing. When Israel's own choices did not include steadfastness to the ways of God (7), He made a further choice, saying through Peter to New Testament saints who were living stones built up a spiritual house, 'but you are a chosen race' (8).

So important to God and central to His purposes was the choice of His earthly race that the whole of the boundaries of all nations were distributed according to its size and number (9). Empires have risen and fallen in relation to their treatment of Israel, and future world allotment will fall in line with the place that God has given to that earthly chosen race (10). What spiritual riches will be apportioned to the spiritual race so chosen (11) could only beggar the imagination now and will have to wait for eternity to reveal. Israel will become to the world what the shekel of the sanctuary was to be to Israel. All things will be commensurate with it. Such is the importance of the choice of God.

Did all the sons of Seth or Shem or Abraham become an integral part of the elect? Not at all! The choice narrowed to the twelve sons of Jacob and their progeny. Not all of Jacob's children were included in this choice (12). Though the word 'race' may emphasize those with a common father, not all who were fathered by any of the patriarchs were included in God's narrow choice. Not even all those who own God as their heavenly Father find themselves included here (13). Many are called; few are chosen (14). The smallness of God's chosen race has always been a stumbling block, even to earnest seekers after God. What a blessing of grace and mercy to ever be considered a part of that which finds its expression in a people who once were none, but are now the people of God (15)!

God impressed upon Israel that their race was chosen in His sovereignty and not because they were anything (16). Through Paul, God also emphasizes that His present choice involves 'not many wise ... mighty ... noble' (17). One purpose in His choosing the weak and beggarly is to prove to all His infinite wisdom and bring to nothing any wisdom so-called that might be arraigned in opposition (18).

From God's choice race, Israel, He was pleased to bring about the natural birth of Christ (19). Unreceived by His own, but received by those called of the Spirit, He is now head of the Church which is His Body; but more than that, Lord of all who will by obedience align themselves with His truth and His people. Chosen in Christ, we are supplied with boundless blessing here and will be hereafter, and here and now are given the inestimable privilege of divine acceptance and service (20) as the 'elect according to the foreknowledge of God the Father, in sanctification of the Spirit, for obedience and sprinkling of the blood of Jesus Christ' (21). As those who firstly know the working of faith, we then become obedient to the Faith (22) and find ourselves linked with that chosen race. Those of Israel who sidestepped their promise to do all that the LORD had said and be obedient would find themselves cut off from the very race to which they by birth had a right. That rule doesn't change.

The purpose for us of God's choice is variously explained. We have looked at Paul's word to the Corinthians about putting to shame those who are wise with this world's wisdom. But Peter expands this by reminding us that we are to "proclaim the excellencies of Him who has called [us] out of darkness into His marvelous light" (23). This we do in a two-pronged thrust, extolling God with our united praises, and proclaiming Christ as the only way of salvation to a sin-weary world.

"Behold, My Servant, whom I uphold; My chosen one in whom My soul delights" (24). Some Bible students say that the 'chosen one' here is Israel, as it seems surely to be in verse 19 of the chapter, but Matthew (12:18-21) makes clear that Messiah is the Servant. Israel was necessary, however, to bring about His natural birth. He was the promised "Star out of Jacob" and will be eventually seen fully as the "Sceptre out of

Israel" (25). But He was to be "the last Adam" (26), the progenitor of a new race.

It is God's will that all men should "be saved and to come to the knowledge of the truth" (27). He makes clear, nonetheless, that all men will not be saved (28); neither, very apparently, will all who are saved come to the knowledge of the truth. Those who are without, God judges (29), and our part is neither to judge nor criticize those who are not among us, but one thing God makes very clear is that those who are obedient to the truth are to be numbered among that chosen race. We are chosen "in [Christ] before the foundation of the world" as far as our salvation is concerned (30). Those who are numbered with this race are also chosen "according to the foreknowledge of God the Father, by the sanctifying work of the Spirit" (31). Our election to obedience to the Faith requires that we make our election more sure (32), a thing that could in no way happen as far as God's election to eternal salvation is concerned.

Through Christ, God's chosen, we who are chosen in Christ know and shall know the abundance of God's grace in all the brilliant aspects of salvation. Through Christ, God's chosen, we who are chosen for a place among God's chosen race, know the blessings of being built up a spiritual house for a holy priesthood and all the blessings of entrance within the veil and drawing near to God in worship (33), Christ is the corner stone to which individuals, being aligned, will also find their place in the alignment of the building, "a dwelling of God in the Spirit", that which "is growing into a holy temple in the Lord" (34).

This realization of God's grace towards us should bring elation, but it must also bring intense humility and a spirit of thankfulness. We are encouraged - indeed, commanded - to ensure a commensurate behaviour towards our fellow saints, each the brother and the sister for whom Christ died, each the brother and the sister that God has chosen to be part of this chosen, holy race.

What, then, have we gleaned? From numbers that surpass human imagination a sovereign God has made choices according to His own wisdom and grace, and each choice has resulted in a decreasing number of chosen ones, until He has at last a chosen race. Those comprising it are all of one Father, are related to each other because of the work of Calvary and an obedience to the faith once for all delivered to the saints. They own Christ as Lord and are built into God's house. In fulfilling their purpose they act concerning God and man, and seek to add to their numbers according to the direction of the Word of God and His Holy Spirit.

The choice of God can be honoured or set aside by those so gathered together, and the appreciation of God's choosing should be a matter of constant praise and consistent humility. The setting aside of the conditions imposed by God can result in expulsion from the race for a time, that there might be repentance, or permanently, should God grant none (35). No greater earthly blessing can be afforded than to be faithful in service among the people of God's chosen race, and heavenly blessings too rich to imagine will forever bless those whose choice is surrendered to God's.

References: (1) E.g. 1 Chron.16:13; Eph.1:4; Ps.33:12 (2) Heb.2:6 (3) Heb.11:8,9,12 (4) Is.40:15-17 (5) Deut.7:6-8 (6) Is.44:1,2 (7) Deut.28:45-47 (8) 1 Pet.2:9 (9) Deut.32:8 (10) Zech.14:17 (11) Eph.2:7 (12) Gen.34:1 (13) 1 Jn.2:19 (14) Matt.22:14 (15) 1 Pet.2:10 (16) Deut.7:7 (17) 1 Cor.1:26 (18) 1 Cor.1:20 (19) Matt.1 (20) 1 Pet.2:5 (21) 1 Pet.1:2 (22) Acts 6:7 (23) 1 Pet.2:9 (24) Is.42:1 (25) Num.24:17 (26) 1 Cor.15:45 (27) 1 Tim.2:4 (28) Rev.20:15 (29) 1 Cor.5:13 (30) Eph.1:4 (31) 1 Pet.1:2 (32) 2 Pet.1:10 (33) Heb.10:19 (34) Eph.2:21,22 (35) 2 Tim.2:25

CHAPTER TWENTY-THREE: QUAKE!

The earthquake that rocked Japan one afternoon was strong enough to actually shift the earth's axis, reported NASA. One effect is that our days are now minutely shorter than they once were. In a sense it shook the whole world's population also, including the complacency of some Christians. This quake, along with what seems to be an increasing number of other natural disasters, unsettles the peace and tranquility of many. In another way, considering the Lord's imminent return, our days are shorter, too! Political turbulence in the Middle East, with wars and rumours of wars and threatened genocide, uneasy and unstable markets the globe around and personal financial stress cause many anxious moments and the searching again of such scriptures as Matthew 24:6-8, where the Lord Jesus said: "... these things must come to pass, but the end is not yet. For nation shall rise against nation ... And there will be famines, pestilences, and earthquakes in various places."

Although "the end is not yet", we also realize that "now our salvation is nearer than when we first believed" (1) (because we are awaiting the return of the Lord to the air, which may occur immediately without any prior signs or further warning). But "all these are the beginning of sorrows". We can't even visualize what the end will feel like. But He also said, "See that you are ['be' in ASV] not troubled" (that is, shaken from your faith.) The Lord had promised the disciples that in the world they would have tribulation. Some of us in western countries have known little of that. There again, the end is not yet!

Perhaps when things take place half a world away we are less bothered than when they occur on our doorsteps, but "fear not" was an expression that the Lord often directed to the insecure even in local distress. The sons of Korah had the correct evaluation:

"God is our refuge and strength, a very present help in trouble. Therefore we will not fear, even though the earth be removed, and though the mountains be carried into the midst of the sea; though its waters roar and be troubled, though the mountains shake with its swelling" (2). And so as believers we have a sure support, but what about those who have not this faith in God and have not the assurance of eternity with Christ? Often, besetting trauma opens an opportunity for a caring act of kindness, a comforting assurance, a gentle word of testimony; and to ourselves a gentle prod of warning: "Therefore, to him who knows to do good and does not do it, to him it is sin" (3). We believers need to take careful note. Generosity with our time and money provides opportunities to spread blessing and the love of God.

Come back to when the deep need is on our doorstep. Not only are the spared ones able to rise to great opportunity for service, but those hardest hit, bereaved, homeless, destitute, even though believers, need to learn the art of gracious acceptance, not only of the trouble, but of relief proffered. In all, earnest prayer and hourly dependence on God and His Word take on a reality that perhaps seemed distant before. Do we really continue to remember those who were so oppressed in last month's news? The troubles continue; so must the prayer of the godly!

Lastly is the opportunity to give "thanks always for all things to God the Father in the name of our Lord Jesus Christ" (4). We appreciate that some who read this need all the help that they can receive, and we can react. We can be really thankful too to know that God is able to bring great blessing even in adversity.

References: (1) Rom.13:11 (2) Ps.46:1-3 (3) Jas.4:17 (4) Eph.5:20

(Bible quotations from NKJV)

CHAPTER TWENTY-FOUR: HOLY LIVING

A doubting disciple once asked a military general what he thought about the possibility of carrying out such commands as evangelizing the whole world, or living a holy life in the midst of a sinful and perverse generation. The general answered that the soldier or the bondservant never asks what is possible: he merely does his utmost to carry out his orders.

What Are Our Orders?

Peter, who had all too profound a knowledge of failure in the matter of holiness, was the apostle used to remind us of the commandment of the Lord (1): "He who called you is holy, you also be holy in all your conduct, because it is written, 'Be holy, for I am holy.'" Peter was quoting from Leviticus 11, a chapter describing rules of conduct for those who as a priesthood followed the LORD. The description found in this chapter nicely defines holiness: separation from the unclean, and separation to the pure. Can those who serve God in priestly capacity today seek anything less than separation from that which defiles and separation to the One who has made us pure? The Christian believer is in a tug-of-war. Satan would separate us from godliness through sin. Christ would separate us from sin to godliness. There is nothing in us naturally that responds to the Lord; there is in each of us a sinful tendency that responds to Satan. Christ alone could say that Satan had nothing in Him. We reflect instead that which Paul felt most deeply: "O wretched man that I am! Who will deliver me from this body of death?" (2). Is it possible in view of our natures to live in the beauty of holiness? What are our orders?

The Secret of Holy Living

Paul tells the Romans and us in Romans 12:1 the secret of holy living: "I beseech you therefore, brethren, by the mercies of God, that you present your bodies a living sacrifice, holy, acceptable to God, which is your reasonable service." He also lets us know that attainment of holy living is a gradual thing demanding constant cleansing from the sinfulness that finds an answer in the 'old man' resident within us (3) and a pressing on to a growing, maturing holiness, a progressing practical sanctification, an increased Christlikeness: "beloved, let us cleanse ourselves from all filthiness of the flesh and spirit, perfecting holiness in the fear of God" (4).

The Holy Spirit's Enabling

The Holy Spirit, so holy, so often grieved and even quenched, works with our spirits to enable us. He loves us and His constraint is the action of divine love. This progression of perfecting holy living is the kind of thing we see in the life of Peter and evidenced in the faithful serenity we observe in the elderly apostle John. Amid unspeakable trials, and given the most moving revelations, they remained serene and immovable. We can observe it also in the lives of godly saints around us, men and women whose experiences, both publicly in life and hidden with the Lord, have developed and are developing in them a quietness and confidence that can be a tremendous source of strength to us all. They purvey for us in their daily walk the qualities of the fruit of the Spirit (5): "love, joy, peace, longsuffering, kindness goodness, faithfulness, gentleness, self-control." And in their imperturbability, they generate quietude. Ancient Joshua gave a prescription and commitment that many readers will already have made personal: "As for me and my house, we will serve the LORD" (6).

Consciously Avoiding Sin

The avoidance of sin should be a very conscious activity in the life of every believer. A life of sanctity is necessitated by our calling: "Only let your conduct be worthy of the gospel of Christ" (7); "walk worthy of the calling with which you were called" (8). And it is prescribed by the future: "Therefore, since all these things will be dissolved, what manner of persons ought you to be in holy conduct and godliness" (9). It is called for because each believer is a temple of the Holy Spirit. It is the evidence of the thing into which we have been called, "a holy temple in the Lord, in whom you also are being built together for a dwelling place of God in the Spirit" (10). God Himself is "glorious in holiness" (11) and everything associated with Him is holy: His Spirit, His house and all in it, His priesthood, His nation, His calling, His Son. To all this we are also called, and to His holiness we must give practical expression. The Lord said He would never leave us nor forsake us (12).

A Recipe for Holy Living

Consider for a moment the holiness of the Son of God. Gabriel commented on it, demons testified to it, those who had seen His walk spoke to God about "Your holy Servant Jesus." He called Himself holy, addressing His Father as, "Holy Father ... We are one." This same One who walks with us, one with us, desires that that walk be a holy one. Paul rejoiced over believers in Rome: "But God be thanked that though you were slaves of sin, yet you obeyed from the heart that form of doctrine to which you were delivered. And having been set free from sin, you became slaves of righteousness" (13). "Slaves of righteousness" - that's the recipe for holy living.

Some Far-reaching Consequences

We don't live to ourselves. The extent of the holiness of my daily living reflects upon the witness of the gospel, the testimony of the saints among whom I live and worship, and upon men's reception of the Lord Himself. Even if my actions remain unobserved by those around who watch, lack of holiness undermines my communion with Christ and affects the spirit of unity with fellow-believers. The old hymn says: "Forgive the sins I now confess to Thee, Forgive the secret sins I cannot see." Constant confession and waiting upon the Lord are necessary tools for the development of holy living.

Building Upon One Another

Perhaps we too often forget or neglect the fact that other believers, fellow-strugglers against all the wiles of the devil, build upon our successes in overcoming the evil one. These little victories in our lives engender strength in others, just as evidence of commonly understood standards of purity and godliness in their lives encourage us in our fruitfulness. We build upon one another. We can also discourage our fellows by our behaviour, like the stone in a house, which displayed characteristics of a plague in Leviticus 14, if the infection were not corrected or the stone removed, the whole building would be infected. A little leaven can affect the whole lump. If we are truly subject to the Lord and His commandments, if the love and care for each other that is enjoined upon us by the Lord is evident, all men will know that we are His disciples and that such discipleship is much to be desired. Christian believers who walk and work with us to a common end will be blessed. Those who did not know subjection and who lacked the love of God in the past caused other people instead to blaspheme (14). How sad if the lack of holiness in my walk should cause such disrespect to God in others!

Traps to Avoid

Of course, there are things to guard against in this matter of trying to live a holy life, traps to avoid. One of them is using a supposed standard of holiness as some sort of self-aggrandizing comparative issue. God took a very dim view of some in Israel who did so, deprecating their behaviour in Isaiah 65:3,5: "A people who provoke Me to anger continually to My face; ... Who say, 'Keep to yourself, do not come near me, for I am holier than you!"

An exemplification of those words was uttered against such people all through Matthew 23. God does not much appreciate those with superior attitudes; folk who compare themselves with others with any kind of disdain in this matter of holiness are hypocrites because any such claim is unholy! Christ never ceased to be holy, yet He ate and drank with sinners; allowed a sinful woman to wash and anoint His feet; spent time with the raving maniac who further defiled himself by running naked amid the tombs. He came to seek and save the lost, and that could not be accomplished by shunning their company, then or now. We serve a God who cares, a Lord to whom all souls matter. Separation does not mean isolation. Like God, we must hate the sin and love the sinner, and we must beware of any hint of a 'holier than thou' attitude. Some have entertained angels unawares. We might wonder just in what form they appeared.

We return to that doubting disciple and his question: Is it possible...? With God all things are possible!

References: (1) 1 Pet.1:15,16 (2) Rom.7:24 (3) 1 Jn.1:8,9 (4) 2 Cor.7:1 (5) Gal.5:22,23 (6) Josh.24:15 (7) Phil.1:27 (8) Eph.4:1 (9) 2 Pet.3:11 (10) Eph.2:21,22 (11) Ex.15:11 (12) Heb.13:5 (13) Rom.6:17,18 (14) Rom.2:24

CHAPTER TWENTY-FIVE: GOSSIP

The Old English word was 'godsibb', a friendly term describing relatives and close friends, and eventually describing the chatter of women gathered to assist in childbirth. The word was first used as a verb by Shakespeare, but its present meaning is quite different, involving the idle and often meaningfully hurtful slanted anecdote that flies on wings of quicksilver and leaves destruction in its path. Solomon described the action as "going down into the inmost body" (1) and he didn't mean with any good results. Paul condemns the actions of such as engage in this hurtful practice: "... idle ... gossips and busybodies, saying things which they ought not" (2). A few in his day were guilty of it; I wonder what he would say if he lived in our time!

Marshall McLuhan described modern gadgets as having become extensions of the human body – the typewriter of the fingers, the bicycle of the legs, the telephone of the ears, and so on. Were he alive today he might expand that thought exponentially. Today, modern gadgetry means we don't even have to wander about from house to house spreading rumours; we can accelerate the practice with the extension of thumb action. We are accountable for the words of our mouths (3); we are no less accountable for the action of our thumbs and fingers! James warns us well: 'If anyone does not stumble in word, he is a perfect man, able also to bridle the whole body ... And the tongue is a fire, a world of iniquity ... it defiles ..." (4). Of course the tongue defiles in many ways, but we need remember that one of them is gossip, whether oral or electronically transmitted!

Among dedicated believers gossip at times disguises itself in the camouflage of "matters for prayer", human interest for supposedly good intent, but nonetheless hurtful in its broadcast. It begins with statements like, "I'm very concerned about ... (you fill in the name)." There are times to speak, but there are times when we need to learn to be silent. One wise man taught his son, "Never overlook the opportunity to keep your mouth shut!" Even prayer meetings should not be used as platforms for gossip. Some things need be prayed about, certainly, but on one's knees, alone with the One who knows all things already (5).

God's law through Moses to Israel was: "You shall not go about as a talebearer among your people ... I am the LORD" (6). To this Solomon adds, 'A talebearer reveals secrets, but he who is of a faithful spirit conceals a matter' (7), and adds in Proverbs 26 that though a talebearer's words are like tasty trifles they cause strife. To the Thessalonian saints Paul exhorts that those who walk in a disorderly manner as busybodies should learn to work in quietness (8).

As well as spreading gossip there is the possibility of feeding on it. Modern media have made celebrity gossip popular and acceptable in our society. No matter what dirt is cast up in the lives of sports stars, celebrities or politicians it becomes a delightful titbit for public consumption on a worldwide scale. Nothing seems taboo; all is open and laid bare – and it defiles! The Christian believer needs no part of it. Gossip is social sewage; it rots the spirit! The Holy Spirit advises us rather to think on things which are true, noble, just, pure, lovely, of good report, things of virtue and praiseworthy (9). The Lord Jesus knew all things, He knew what was in man, but He didn't talk about it, nor did He advise the spread of that kind of news. He should be our example in word as well as action. He did not gossip; can we who are His afford or even want to do so?

(Bible quotations from NKJV)

References: (1) Prov.18:8; 26:22 (2) 1 Tim.5:13 (3) Matt.12:36 (4) Jas.3:2,6 (5) Matt.6:6 (6) Lev.19:16 (7) Prov.11:13 (8) 2 Thess.3:11-12 (9) Phil.4:8

CHAPTER TWENTY-SIX: MAKING DISCIPLES

Our Charge and Focus

The spiritual growth of churches of God depends on various conditions; the numerical growth that we long to see is dependent largely on disciples making disciples. The charge of the Lord Jesus Christ to His disciples was:

> "Go therefore and make disciples of all the nations, baptizing them in the name of the Father and of the Son and of the Holy Spirit, teaching them to observe all things that I have commanded you" (1).

They were to go as sent ones (2), assured of the presence of the Lord Jesus (3); they were sent as the Father had sent Him, a Lamb into the midst of wolves (4); they would need a heart-yearning for souls that would drive them on though death threatened (5), and an urgency in the task ahead, knowing that the time was short (6). They were the few who turned the world upside-down (7). They preached and made disciples and churches were planted and carried on the work both locally and on a broader scope (8). The early Christian believers were intensely focused on their task. Christian believers in churches of God today will need similar intensity motivated by the love of God, an intense desire not only for numerical increase, but also to fulfil the Lord's commandment.

Paul told the Corinthians that, "Knowing, therefore, the terror of the Lord, we persuade men," (9) for he realized that he must stand at the Judgement Seat of Christ to answer for deeds done in the body, but he also said, "the love of Christ compels us" (10). A healthy desire not to disappoint the Master and a great love for Him and His desires are sound motivation for soul-winning. The wise win souls, (11) and the heart of wisdom searches for the direction of the Spirit of God as to where and how to fulfil the directive. Scripture indicates that God does not necessarily work everywhere at once (12). A wise piece of advice that I have tried to follow is to try to work where the Lord gives evidence that He is working, rather than asking the Lord to bless where I think He should, perhaps having received no indication that that is the place or circumstance of His choice.

Defining Discipleship

But once souls are saved they are to be directed towards discipleship. What is it? A disciple is simply a learner. Moses had his disciples, as did John the Baptist, as does the Lord Jesus. We learn from Him through His Word, by the direction of the Holy Spirit, and through teachers that He has appointed who rightly divide the Word of truth and break it down for us. Evidence of divine appointment is seen in their effectiveness as teachers and in their strict adherence to the Word as to what is taught. Teachers find assurance about their particular ability from the appreciation and recognition of their brethren. There are, of course, false teachers (13). We must be careful from whom we learn. What do we learn? To follow the teaching, rather than the teacher. What will that teaching involve? All the truth (14).

The rules of living under the Old Covenant were called the law; the rules of living under the New Covenant are called the faith or the truth. These will involve showing out the various characteristics of Christ outlined by Paul as the fruit of the Spirit (15). As well as behavioural attributes they will include such vital components as reading and meditation on the Word, prayer, baptism, fellowship with like-minded believers, keeping the Lord's commandments concerning the breaking of the bread, and a willingness to learn to make more disciples.

This whole learning procedure is gradual. Paul, learned man in the Scriptures as he was, firstly went to the desert of Arabia to learn about Christ, His Person and His will, before the Spirit thrust him into what was to be his life work (16). Those who successfully evangelize today will need to 'learn Christ' before trying to inculcate that teaching in others. And when we are ready, where do we start?

Our Starting Point

We love our families and all who are given to us by blood relationship. They are one of the greatest areas of outreach available to us, and they are so near us. The family is also Satan's target for some of his fiercest conflict. If Satan can hold onto our families he has greatly reduced our own effectiveness by discouragement. Making disciples starts here, with prayer, example, words wisely spoken and earnest expectation of a success aimed at by directing our children toward goals that will not conflict with discipleship. We live in a world that espouses success at almost any price; many educational pursuits might direct our children away from the pathway of discipleship. Mothers, as those who normally spend more time with their young, particularly need prayer support as they give earnest attention to this part of busy motherhood.

Then we have friends and neighbours who need to hear the Word. One company of believers has a sign that is read as you leave their meeting place parking lot: You are now entering the mission field! While the whole world beckons, we need to remember that salvation is offered freely to those that are near at hand as well as those who are far off. Pray the Lord of the harvest that He will send forth labourers into His harvest, but you must be prepared to fill a little place if God be glorified.

Our Urgency and Breadth of Vision

Both individual disciples and the collective entity, churches of God, need to feel the urgency of reaching the lost. Our time, at best, is limited and souls enter eternity by the minute. Some in churches of God have been gifted with a passion and ability for evangelism (17). These need to be supported in prayer and financially by those in the home base of local assemblies as they go out in this vital work of making disciples. Paul said that it was God's will that all should be saved and come to the knowledge of the truth, and to this end he was both a preacher and a teacher, a preacher of the Gospel, a teacher of the truth (18).

The early apostles were sent out with all the world as their eventual target (19). The aim of the disciple today must also include this worldwide vision. Where our feet may not go, our voices and our printed material can certainly penetrate. We shall be gratified as we see God using such means of broadcasting the seed to bring forth abiding fruit to His glory. As on the pillars before the temple there is hidden fruit as well as visible (Jeremiah 52:23 NASB): that eternity alone will reveal.

One of our most fruitful works has been among children and youth. Years after the work seems to be completed and young ones have moved on, the lives of the taught ones can exhibit the desired effect, and in many cases adults testify gladly to the blessings of the Sunday school or week night class, or to the camp work or follow-up effort.

The Secret of Disciple-making

The often unseen powerhouse of disciple-making resulting in church growth begins in the secret place where godly saints pray for the lost and those who endeavour to win them. In private, this is often a function of older sisters, women who have been drawn close to the

Lord through life's hardships, women who have a very vital part of the work that brings God glory. This partnership in prayer is not limited to any group of believers in the church, and the church itself will grow in relation to its prayer life. The prayer meeting of a growing church will exhibit vitality and faithfulness. It is the arena where many a spiritual battle is won. Eternity alone will reveal the part that praying souls have had in any victory for the Master. Brethren also need to learn to wait upon the Lord for clear direction as to just where to work. While it is true that we are to sow beside all waters, it is manifestly true that we might better seek the Lord's face as to where He is working than supplicating Him on behalf of our own ideas as to where we think He should be working.

Someone has said that to do the same things over and over and to expect different results is futile. If the things we do are the result of tradition or bygone success, there is a need to look to the Lord for ways to change our outreach that do not in any way circumvent His will. Where what we do is laid down for us in the Word, we must strictly adhere to it. Finally, in spite of a becoming humble attitude about what we are engaged in, saints should not be reticent to share information about their involvement in evangelistic work. With knowledge others may pray intelligently about the effort, bringing help for the witness and glorifying God in the process.

References: (1) Matt.28:19,20 (2) Jn.20:21 (3) Matt.28:20 (4) Matt.10:16 (5) 2 Cor.11:23 (6) 2 Cor.6:2 (7) Acts 17:6 (8) 1 Thess.1:8 (9) 2 Cor.5:11 (10) 2 Cor.5:14 (11) Prov.11:30 (12) Acts 16:7 (13) 2 Cor.11:13-15 (14) Jn.16:13 (15) Gal.5:22,23 (16) Gal.1:16,17 (17) Eph.4:11 (18) 1 Tim.2:4,7 (19) Mk.16:15

CHAPTER TWENTY-SEVEN: THE CHOSEN SERVANT

"Behold, My Servant, whom I uphold;

My chosen one in whom My soul delights.

I have put My Spirit upon Him;

He will bring forth justice to the nations.

He will not cry out or raise His voice,

Nor make His voice heard in the street.

A bruised reed He will not break

And a dimly burning wick He will not extinguish;

He will faithfully bring forth justice.

He will not be disheartened or crushed

Until He has established justice in the earth;

And the coastlands will wait expectantly for His law." (1)

Isaiah makes four references to Christ as the Servant of the LORD ('Yahweh') (2); this is the first. Some Bible scholars have seen this as a reference to Israel, some to Cyrus, some to Isaiah himself or to the prophets as a group. They use such verses as Isaiah 41:8; 42:19; 49:3 and 49:5 as justification for their hypotheses, but Matthew 12:15-21 makes very clear that Isaiah's prophecy here is fulfilled in the Lord Jesus Christ. No other individual or nation could have shown the tenderness and restraint necessary, nor fulfilled the mandate to establish justice in the world, try as they might.

Christ alone (on whom the Spirit not only came, but rested and moved Him in everything He did) was upheld by His God throughout His whole earthly existence. He alone is God's chosen vessel, never failing or discouraged, no matter what trials and temptations Satan might put in His way, until God's kingdom is come, universal justice is established, His will is done on earth as it is in heaven. To display His tenderness and grace Christ took on Himself the form of a servant (3), serving God and man, coming not to be served, but to serve (4), and to give His life as a ransom: 'Pattern Servant, doing all God's will below' (5).

At the cross men jeered at the Lord Jesus: "Commit yourself to the LORD; let Him deliver him; let Him rescue him, because He delights in him" (6). The question remains: if He was unique in all His ways, peerless, incomparable, daily the Father's delight, why was He the One chosen? The task to set things straight in all the earth involved the Calvary experience, being emptied, enslaved, humbled, obedient even to death on the cross. The simple answer is that He was the only one who was worthy (7). And to accomplish the work, God upheld Him, took firm hold of Him and kept Him upright (8); God would not leave Him alone (9) and even in punishing Him for sin would feel every blow delivered.

God would sustain Him in every endeavour, even to the bringing of justice to the Gentiles. The choice involved supplying Him with all divine power in giving Him the fullness of the Spirit. His Father bore testimony to that choice on the Mount of Transfiguration: "This is My Son, My Chosen One" (10). He was "rejected by men, but is choice and precious in the sight of God" (11). Marvel of marvels: He was the Chosen One long before the foundation of the earth, and we, through divine grace and mercy, were chosen in Him that we should be "holy and blameless before Him" (12)! He came for the consolation of Israel, anointed to bring good news to the afflicted, but He was also "a light of revelation to the Gentiles" (13). For this He would not surrender any of the attributes of deity, but would assume the limitations of humanity and the setting aside of some of His divine prerogatives during the period of His time on earth.

The Lord Jesus Christ was, and is, God's Chosen One; there was no one else who could accomplish the divine will. Through obedience and self-denial in voluntary submission to the Father (for He was in every sense on equality with God) He won sovereignty over all people and things; to Him alone has been given all judgment (14); He is the only one in heaven or on earth worthy of such honour (15); He was the only one slain for all mankind and resurrected from the dead in victory (16). His obedience and self-denial are also an example of godliness to all who are chosen and elect in Him. Wherefore God has given Him the name above every name, the place high over all (17).

References: (1) Is.42:1-4 (NASB) (2) Is.42:1-4; 49:1-6; 50:4-11; 52:13-53:12 (3) Phil.2:7 (4) Matt.20:28 (5) C. Belton PHSS 3 (6) Ps.22:8 (7) Rev.5:4-5 (8) Keil and Delitzsch, Commentary on the Old Testament: Isaiah, (Chapter 42, verse 1) p.175: "Tamakh b' means to lay firm hold of and keep upright." (9) Jn.16:32 (10) Lk.9:35 (11) 1 Pet.2:4 (12) Eph.1:4 (13) Lk.2:32 (14) Jn.5:22; Acts 10:42; 17:31 (15) Rev.5:5 (16) Rev.5:9 (17) Phil.2:9-11

CHAPTER TWENTY-EIGHT: PRAISE IN PRAYER

Prayer and praise accomplish many things. Besides the sweetness of communion, the cleansing of confession, the reassurance of care and deliverance, the fellowship of those with whom and for whom we pray and the development of patience and steadfastness within ourselves, there is the tremendous uplift of spirit and strengthening of all our parts that comes to individuals and groups who give themselves to praise to God and waiting upon the Lord.

Great men and women of God and the people of God in their strength have always dedicated themselves to prayer and its highly important aspect, praise. Godly saints today do likewise. The corporate praise of the assembly as it joins with the people of God in holy priesthood service is both a duty and a delight, filling the hands of Him who as our High Priest presents our adoration perfectly to His God and Father, and as a by-product, fills the participants with an exhilaration of spirit that levels the steep inclines of the mundane. Mounting up "with wings like eagles" becomes the reality of the life of the obedient disciple; "running unwearied" the experience of the faithful (Is.40:31).

Someone has said that if the Scriptures are the jewelled setting that God has placed on earth for our delight, the Psalms are the precious centre stone. These are filled with the heart's deepest yearnings. We wish to examine a few that express the heart's overflowing in praise; the bubbling over of the cup of exceeding joy. Just to read the writers' exuberance in such psalms as 103, 107, 113 and 145-150 fills the human spirit with the longing that the sons of Korah expressed when they likened their desire to the panting hart for the water brooks (Ps.42:1), and Swain, the hymn-writer, enjoyed as he looked forward to eternal song: 'On earth the song begins, In heaven more sweet and loud ...'

The profundity of one's being is affected as we exult in the power and majesty of the One who has accomplished all things. "Bless the LORD, O my soul; And all that is within me ..." (Ps.103:1). We are stirred to the depths as we soar to the heights, not in a momentary poetic euphoria, but in lasting, spiritual refreshment. Oh, that it would occur even more often!

The Psalms are often categorized into groups according to similar features for study purposes. Among these are psalms of declarative praise, beginning with expressions such as, "I will praise ...", followed by the reason why, a renewed vow of praise and ending with some instruction for others and/or examples. Psalms that call upon others to praise the Lord and develop an illustrated reason, followed by a new exhortation to such thankfulness usually fall into the category of descriptive praise and are really hymns of deeply-rooted joy and appreciation. But it's not the dryness of the categories in which we might place psalms for study purposes, but the great confidence in the Lord of the writers, the spontaneous and earnest enjoyment they had in God, and the encouragement to saints of all ages to enter into the praise of His glory that makes us feel in a special way the message of the Spirit to us and through us in our worship.

Psalm 103 leads to appreciation of covenant blessings and so finds a special place in the hearts of those under New Covenant relationship with God. The mercies of forgiveness, healing, enrichment, compassion, faithfulness and renewed vigour, all given with an appreciation of and allowance for our human frailty, call upon us to respond in exultation, thanking God for His eternal love: "Bless the LORD, O my soul; And all that is within me, bless His holy name!" (Ps.103:1) Who could read the Psalm and not be thoroughly enthralled with His goodness; and fail to obey the exhortation to copious praise?

Psalm 107, possibly written during the Babylonian captivity, calls upon the redeemed of the Lord to appreciate the deliverance of the people of God, and His concern for their constant health and safety. It gives a call to express their praise in the solemn assembly. To all God's mercy is added His evident power, not only over nature, but over all their experiences, and for this he writes: "Oh, that men would give thanks to the LORD for His goodness, and for His wonderful works to the children of men! Let them exalt Him also in the assembly of the people, and praise Him in the company of the elders" (Ps. 107:31,32).

Sung each year before the Passover, and first of the Hallel (that collection of praise which was to be sung at the great festivals of Israel and consisted of Psalms 113-118) Psalm 113 is a nice connection between the praise of Hannah as she rejoiced in the Lord for His kindness in the birth of Samuel (1 Sam.2:1-10), and the song of Mary who exulted at the promise of the coming Messiah (Lk.1:46-55). It begins and ends with 'Praise the LORD!' and well it might, for it relates the majesty and condescension of deity, even to the gracious intervention in the lives of the poor of the refuse heap who cling to it for the warmth of its fires and for eked-out food and clothing.

It raises the lowly from there to sit with the princes of His people. He is One who listens to the pleas of those barren, who, Hannah-like, long for the richer blessing of a home where she can be the mother of children. The writer calls for praise in our own day, for God has granted us who were spiritually equally barren an "inheritance of the saints in the light" (Col.1:12). We sit at the Lord's table (1 Cor.10:21)! Hallelujah!

From Psalm 136 echo twenty-six refrains extolling the loyal love (Hebrew: 'hesed') of God, His creation, all the aid and deliverance that has been vouchsafed to His people and His abundant grace in opening His hand to feed every creature. We are enjoined to give thanks to "the God of heaven". That title is mentioned only here in the Psalms, but elsewhere, twenty-three times. He made heaven, is in heaven, rules from heaven. The Son came from heaven that we might go there, and has made us meantime citizens of that place. "Oh, give thanks to the God of heaven! For His mercy endures forever" (Ps.136:26). No wonder this 136th psalm is referred to as the 'Great Hallel'.

Of course, every believer in the Lord Jesus has cause to praise the Lord, but the psalms here speak of the added exultation that is the delight of His own peculiar people collectively. It is the nation that has known such grace and blessing; it is the nation that should be bursting with His praise.

In the final six psalms in the psalter the word 'praise' leaps out at us forty-three times. Psalm 145, however, is the only one in the book that is entitled 'A Psalm of Praise' (Hebrew: 'tehillah'). David is thrilled with the fact that God's mighty acts could be lauded from generation to generation, yet no one had to that time, or has since, really risen to the greatness of praise commensurate with His mighty works. The fact that His kingdom is everlasting foretells a continuance of the gratitude of His own. God is righteous and God is loving, therefore all should call upon Him and all should give Him praise, meditating on the glorious splendour of His majesty and speaking of the power of His awesome acts.

Psalms 146 to 150, although anonymous as far as we are concerned, continue along similar lines to David in 145. It was no doubt these psalms that inspired Lady Cockburn-Campbell to pen the words we often sing in worship:

> Praise ye Jehovah, praise the Lord most holy,

CALLED AS WE ARE

Who cheers the contrite, girds with strength the weak;

Praise Him who will with glory crown the lowly,

And with salvation beautify the meek.

Praise ye the Lord for all His loving-kindness,

And all the tender mercies He has shown;

Praise Him who pardons all our sins and blindness,

And calls us sons and takes us for His own.

The wonders that moved the psalmists and move us are catalogued in these last six hymns of praise, some of which are: "The LORD upholds all who fall, and raises up all who are bowed down" (1). "The LORD is near to all who call upon Him in truth ... He also will hear their cry and save them" (2). "The LORD gives freedom to the prisoners" (3). "The LORD opens the eyes of the blind" (4). "The LORD ... relieves the fatherless and widow" (5). "He heals the brokenhearted and binds up their wounds" (6). "The LORD lifts up the humble" (7). "The LORD takes pleasure in His people; He will beautify the humble with salvation" (8).

Meditation upon the wonders of the LORD will fill our hearts with praises. Resulting praise to God in the congregation, like the ointment of pure nard, will fill the whole house with His fragrance (Jn.12:3). He is worthy to be praised. Praise the LORD!

References: 1) Ps.145:14 2) Ps.145:18,19 3) Ps.146:7 4) Ps.146:8 5) Ps.146:9 6) Ps.147:3 7) Ps.47:6 8) Ps.149:4

CHAPTER TWENTY-NINE: CHRIST IN MATTHEW'S GOSPEL

Each Gospel writer presents the Lord Jesus Christ from a different perspective. Matthew, whose writing tends to be organized thematically rather than chronologically, arranges his Gospel around five great discourses of the Lord (1). He also relies heavily on Old Testament quotations, using them about fifty times and referring to that book an additional seventy-five. This particularly suits his purpose to relate to his Jewish audience that the Jesus of whom he wrote was none other than the "seed of Abraham" through whom all the nations of the earth would be blessed and the direct descendent of David who must eventually occupy the throne. Matthew was particularly suited to write his book having been a tax-gatherer and having to keep careful records (2).

Once Matthew had been called by the Lord to discipleship, he prepared a feast for his former colleagues and invited Jesus as the honoured guest, no doubt to introduce them to the Saviour (3). This kind of intensity also displays itself in the work that he was called to accomplish by the Holy Spirit in his writing.

Micah had prophesied the place of Christ's birth and the fact that He would be ruler in Israel (4). Matthew goes about proving this by dividing his book into six sections, each one finishing with words such as, "And when Jesus finished these words or finished giving instructions or finished these parables" (5). Each section proves Jesus to be the Messiah, the sent One from God, the King.

Concentrating largely on the oral teachings of the Lord, Matthew shows clearly the answer to the question plaguing the Jews of his day:

"If this is the King, where is His kingdom?" While God's kingdom takes a different form in this age, David's throne will be seen to be eternally established in a future time when Christ returns to this earth to confirm His rule and authority. Matthew is the only Gospel writer to mention the 'church' and to show the nature of discipline within it in Christ's present realm on earth (6). He also proves over and over that this One fulfils the prophecies and promises of the Old Testament, citing again and again "that it might be fulfilled" (7).

Matthew has been called the Gospel of the King. Not only does the writing begin with ancestral tracing back to David, the Magi from the east come inquiring, "Where is He who has been born King of the Jews?" (8). Eight times over Matthew ascribes the regal title "Son of David" to the Saviour (9), he relates the fulfilment of Zechariah's prophecy about the triumphal entry with all its kingly significance (10) and tells Jesus' own words about His future reign (11): "... then [the Son of Man] will sit on His glorious throne." Jesus is asked by Pilate, "Are you the king of the Jews?" to which He answers, "It is as you say" (12).

Over the cross of Christ is written, "THIS IS JESUS THE KING OF THE JEWS" (13). This is the One who said, "'All authority has been given to Me in heaven and on earth ..." (14). The whole book is arranged around Jesus as King: His birth as king of the Jews, His preparation for kingship, His power, His kingdom, His kingly mission, His kingly entry into Jerusalem, the future kingdom, the death and resurrection of the King and the great commission of the King and kingdom.

The day is hastening when Christ will be revealed, King of the Jews, King of the nations, King of kings. This is Matthew's Messiah and King, the Saviour of the Jews, and, thankfully, our Saviour and King also (15).

References: (1) Matt.5-7;10;13;18;24-25 (2) Matt.9:9 (3) Lk.5:29-32; Matt.9:10 (4) Mic.5:2 (5) Matt.7:28; 11:1; 13:53; 19:1; 26:1 (6) Matt.16:18; 18:17 (7) NKJV e.g. Matt.2:23 (8) Matt.2:2 (9) Matt.1:1; 9:27; 12:23; 15:22; 20:30, 31; 21:9,15 (10) Matt.21:1-11 (11) Matt.25:31 (12) Matt.27:11 (13) Matt.27:37 (14) Matt.28:18 (15) Matt.28:19-20

CHAPTER THIRTY: THE ERROR OF MONARCHIANISM

The errors of Monarchianism (from the Greek 'mono' – one, and 'arche' – rule) are misunderstandings about the nature of God that began in the second century A.D. They take several different forms, but the two main groups are:

1. The modalistic theory – that God is not a Trinity of Persons, but one Person operating in three different modes as Father, Son, and Holy Spirit alternatively, and

2. The dynamic monarchianist theory – that God is One, above all others indivisible and of one nature and that Jesus Christ was not co-eternal with the Father, but a man, who because of His perfect life, wonderful love and sinlessness was adopted by God at the time of His baptism or ascension, becoming God at one of those particular times.

Those who accept these teachings also hold that the Holy Spirit is not a divine person, but a force or presence of the one God, the Father.

Emanuel Swedenborg in the early 1600s propounded a variation of modalistic monarchianism, asserting that God is one divine Person whose name is Jesus Christ. Swedenborgianism, also known as The New Church or The Church of New Jerusalem is active in Canada and the USA today, but has a negligible presence in the UK. It believes that salvation does not come through the atoning work of Jesus Christ, but by the adherent practising faithfully whatever religion he accepts as true. In essence that means that it doesn't matter what one believes so long as one is faithful to one's own beliefs. In other words, man gets to declare his own rules for salvation, service and eternity. Other present-day adherents to modalistic beliefs are the Oneness Pentecostal groups known as United Pentecostals and the United Apostolic churches. Jehovah's Witnesses, Christadelphians and Unitarians hold to the dynamic monarchianistic viewpoint: Christ is not God the Son and the Spirit of God is nothing but an influence, a power of God for good.

It seems that wherever believers in God disagree with the clear teaching of Scripture their differences will centre on some aspect of the Lord Jesus Christ and salvation through faith in Him and His finished work at Calvary, Satan ever attempting to discredit and dishonour Him and make the work of Calvary of little or no effect and the gracious working of God the Spirit of little consequence.

But what does Scripture say? It is true that the 'Great Shema' of Israel plainly states "Hear, O Israel! The LORD is our God, the LORD is one!" (1) and that, backed up by the Lord's own quoting of the verse in Mark 12:29, has been misinterpreted by many to discredit the teaching of the Trinity. It is true that while the Hebrew plural 'Elohim' of Genesis 1:1 does not necessarily insist on God being a Trinity, the Hebrew plural often signifying majesty of character rather than plurality of numbers, but it most certainly leaves room for the concept of a Trinity. New Testament Scriptures link the three persons as equal: each one is God indivisible, yet each separate from the other two. Matthew 28:19 shows them linked under one name, the name of the Father and the Son and the Holy Spirit.

The three are again linked by Paul: "The grace of the Lord Jesus Christ, and the love of God, and the fellowship of the Holy Spirit, be with you all" (2). Again in 1 Corinthians 12:4-6, when speaking of spiritual gifts, Paul links the three. Hebrews 10:29-31 shows the severity of punishment due to any who discredit the work of the Son and the

Holy Spirit. And Peter in his first epistle (3) again displays the triune God working together in unity in connection with His New Testament people, speaking of the foreknowledge of God, the sanctification of the Spirit and the blood of sprinkling of Jesus Christ.

Scripture shows the Trinity to be co-equal, co-eternal and consubstantial. Monarchianism undermines the deity of the Lord Jesus Christ and likewise questions the existence of the Holy Spirit as a Person at all, much less one of the Trinity. John 1:1 shows Christ as one with God from eternity (4) and yet separate in personality, Himself God the creator of all things and life-giver apart from whom there can be no life nor life eternal. Thomas had the correct appreciation when he said of Christ: "My Lord, and my God!" (5). Even God the Father acknowledges Him on several occasions saying, "This is my beloved Son" (6) and again in Hebrews 1:8 the Father states: "But of the Son He says, "Your throne, O God, is forever and ever." Paul rightly described the Lord Jesus to the Colossians: "He is the image of the invisible God, the firstborn of all creation. For by Him all things were created ... He is before all things, and in Him all things hold together" (7). To this he adds: "For in Him all the fullness of Deity dwells in bodily form" (8). The seriousness of believing otherwise is underlined by the Lord Himself in John 8:24: "... unless you believe that I am He, you will die in your sins." The result of that is seen in verse 21: "... where I am going, you cannot come." Hebrews 1:3 linked with Philippians 2:6-11 should clinch the matter with regard to scriptural foundation: Jesus Christ is not only the Son of God; He is God the Son.

The Spirit, too, is God and a separate Person of the godhead. He displays all the attributes of personality: He is an advocate (9); He is a comforter (10); He has a mind (11); He can be insulted (12); He can be lied to (13); He exercises a will in accordance with the Father and the Son (14); He delights in the depths of God and the Son, not only searching them, but revealing them to those who seek God in His

Word (15). God alone can be blasphemed, as He was, and the Spirit is outright called God in Acts 5:3-4, as He is in 2 Corinthians 3:17-18: "the Lord, the Spirit." He is eternal (16); omnipresent (17); omniscient (18); God alone is good, and Nehemiah 9:20 calls Him God's good Spirit. Many more verses might be added to declare His personality and His deity. What abundant grace on His part to dwell within us!

References: (1) Deut.6:4 (2) 2 Cor.13:14 (3) 1 Pet.1:2 (4) Mic.5:2 (5) Jn.20:28 (6) Matt.3:17; Matt.17:5 (7) Col.1:15-17 (8) Col.2:9 (9) Rom.8:26 (10) Jn.14:16 (11) Rom.8:27 (12) Heb.10:29 (13) Acts 5:3 (14) Jn.16:13 (15) 1 Cor.2:10-11 (16) Heb.9:14 (17) Ps.139:7,10 (18) 1 Cor.2:10-11

CHAPTER THIRTY-ONE: SONS OF THE MIGHTY

David's cave became David's stronghold, and mighty men gathered to him there. Among them were eleven sons of Gad. Their faces were like the faces of lions, and they were like gazelles upon the mountains. Men of valor, trained for war, they could handle shield and spear. The of least of them was equal to a hundred of their enemies, and the greatest was equal to a thousand, and they gathered with others until there was an army like the army of God. Where would there be a human army equal to that?

When they met and were fed there was great joy in Israel (1 Chr.12:40). But they acknowledged one that was even greater. "You are worth ten thousand of us", they said to David. Where would there be a greater than he? David, in turn, placed himself in proper relationship to that One, saying, "The LORD said to my Lord ... David then calls Him Lord" (Matt.22:44,45). Who then is this One? He is the One who prophetically is described as "outstanding among ten thousand" (Songs 5:10), as wholly desirable, as altogether lovely (5:16). He is greater than angels (Heb.1:6) and He is fairer than the sons of men (Is.45:2). Reuben, eldest son of the patriarch, Jacob, had this spoken of him: "Reuben, you are my first-born; My might and the beginning of my strength, preeminent in dignity and preeminent in power. Uncontrolled as water, you shall not have pre-eminence" (Gen.49:3,4).

But of One who was poured out like water, God says: "... He is the image of the invisible God, the firstborn of all creation ... so that He Himself might come to have first place in everything ... For it was the Father's good pleasure for all the fulness to dwell in Him" (Col.1:15,19). And what is our relationship to such a One? "... He is not ashamed to call them brethren" (Heb.2:11). "For all who are being led by the Spirit of God, these are sons of God", says Romans 8:14, "sons of the mighty". It is not known whether David had the sons of the tribe of Gad in mind when he penned Psalm 29, or whether he was thinking about angels. He calls for the "sons of the mighty" to "ascribe to the LORD" the glory due to His Name (v.1), and to "worship the LORD in holy array" (v.2). Everything in His Temple says, "Glory!" (v.9). Verse 1 is translated "Worship the LORD in the beauty of holiness" in the Revised Version.

The meaning is likely that we are to worship the Lord for the splendour of His holiness. For the sons of the mighty take on the character of the One they worship. Valiant men, those trained for the day, still gather to the place where our David is, to take on His likeness, His character. He is Son over God's house. And wherever He is, is a stronghold.

CHAPTER THIRTY-TWO: MOSES THE MAN OF GOD - CHOSEN, PREPARED AND CALLED

Moses, the seventh from Abraham, was the son of Amram and Jochebed, Amram being the grandson of Levi. He was the third of three children, all of whom would be used together to lead the people of God. From birth his life was in jeopardy by human standards, beginning with the threat of a Nile grave by the edict of a wicked Pharaoh. However, the whole tribe of Levi had been chosen by God for priestly service within His house.

Moses had been chosen not only as their leader, but as the leader of all the people, and there was not a force in this world or any other that could undermine God's sovereignty. Ironically enough, through the direction of God, Moses knew the protection of the king and the luxury of his palace. Even his mother was paid to care for him and teach him, all this through the moving of the tender heart of the princess, the daughter of the wicked Pharaoh. God is absolute in His sovereignty. None can stay His hand or question His wisdom. But within the parameters of His overall purposes He makes room for the operation of the human will of the men and women involved and receives praise and glory through their faithfulness.

Those who are chosen by God might have to endure hardship and threats, may know what it is to be lonely or despised, but God's chosen ones will be protected so as to fulfil their calling - in Moses' day or in ours. God prepares those whom He has chosen for the service that He has appointed, and Moses was no exception. He was educated in all the protocol of the royal palace, a knowledge that would no doubt benefit

Moses one day, but he was also educated in all the learning of Egypt (6) and some of that he would have to unlearn.

Forty years in the wilderness in all the hardships of the desert would enhance his dependence upon the God he would serve, and even the strength and authority he wielded there he must surrender to the One in whom rests all authority, all power. The arm that slew the offending Egyptian (7) must be seen to be undependable in its own strength and God caused momentary leprosy and rejuvenation under a new power (8).

With a rod he had fearlessly met the threats of the desert with his flock, but even that rod would become useless and fearful before him as a menacing serpent, though taken again contrary to nature, for he grasped it by the tail, a thing he would know not to do (9) for a sudden writhing of the beast would bring poisonous fangs home with deadly accuracy. Moses would learn to trust without question if he were to wield the rod of God among His people. His shoes, the sign of his authority, must be laid aside in appreciation of the holiness (10) of the One who dwelt in the thorn bush (11).

Even his family over which he ruled as head would be for a time taken from him so that he might really rely on the presence of his God. Moses, learning the lessons, would one day walk where no man had ever yet dared to walk, unique in his leadership, speaking to the God of glory face to face (12). The lessons of unlearning, learning, surrender and submission must be learnt by all who would come into the presence of God in holy array!

When the right time came, Moses, who must have put from his mind the conviction that he had once cherished, that he would be a deliverer of his people (13), was called by God to be just that. It was not by his own might or as knowledge, but by humility, obedience, and in the assurance of the fullness of the presence of the I AM, in whom was all knowledge and authority.

It is notable that the presence of the great I AM should dwell in a thorn bush and speak from it. Thorns were associated with something so altogether contrary to the holiness of God (14). But that same deity would one day take on himself the form of one under the same curse of sin, though He Himself was sinless, and would wear a crown of thorns upon His peerless brow. And from there God speaks today (15) so that we who are chosen and in measure prepared, might meet a further preparation and calling to the holiness and appointed task of God, whether that be as a leader of God's people, or one joined hand in hand and one in purpose with those so called, as were Miriam and Aaron.

I suppose Moses asked his question out of some humility and feeling of unworthiness, "Who am I?" (17). But it was the wrong question. The important one followed, "Who are You?". And in the answer to that, that the self-existent and eternal I AM was the One in command, all the difference lies.

Natural reticence can be a demonstration of honest humility, but not when it stands contrary to the commandment of God. Unwillingness to speak out might be born of shyness, but it must not countermand the authority of the One who made man's mouth. On Moses' part, the faith that had brought him thus far must grow to surpass the threats of seas and armies, wilderness and wilfulness, until seemingly lonely and alone he must ascend Pisgah, unable to accompany his people to even greater victory, unaware that what he was suffering was the target of cosmic interest (19).

What do we learn from all this? What are the lessons that we can apply today right where we live in our own circumstances? The God who made choices before the earth was framed that we should be His bondservants and share His glory (20), who has promised His presence through any wilderness experience (21), also wants to prepare us and call us to great things for Himself. Anything commanded by and fulfilled for Him is a great thing - good works afore prepared that we should walk in them (22). But first must come an emptying of self, a relying on Him whom we see though invisible (23), and a determination to follow to the letter the commandments that He has laid down for us in His Word.

Doing that, we can have the expectation of powers wrought powerless (24), of deliverances thought impossible (25) of seas melting away before us, and of mountains scaled and rescaled, bringing us closer into the purpose and presence of God. Moses was one day drawn from the waters of judgement and made to stand in the very presence of the God of glory! Can we see ourselves in this as those chosen, prepared and called? Christian, today you can exult in the addition of 'justified' and 'glorified' (26)!

References: (1) Num.26:59 (2) Micah 6:4; Num.12:3; 6-8 (3) Deut.21:5 (4) Ex.3:14 (5) Ex.2:6-10 (6) Acts 7:22 (7) Acts 7:24 (8) Ex.4:6-7 (9) Ex.4:4 (10) Ex.3:5 (11) Acts 7:35 (12) Deut.4:10; Num.12:8 (13) Acts 7:25 (14) Gen.3:18 (15) Heb.1:2 (16) Heb.13:17 (17) Ex3:11 (18) Ex.3:11 (19) Jude v.9 (20) Eph.1:4;Col.1:3.4 (21) Matt.28:20 (22) Eph.2:10 (23) Heb.11:27 (24) Eph.6:13 (25) Acts 12:6-12 (26) Rom.8:30

CHAPTER THIRTY-THREE: CHOICES

The wilful person, for the moment, has lots of choice; the obedient servant of God may have none. Lot was offered abundant opportunity for himself and his herdsmen. "Lot chose for himself all the valley of the Jordan" (Gen.13:11). Abraham had no choice but to be obedient. Joshua asked the people whether they would serve the Lord or "the gods which your father served which were beyond the River, or the gods of the Amorites in whose land you are living' (Josh. 24:15). Elijah challenged Israel as to whether they would follow the Lord or Baal (1 Kin.18:21). To that point they had an option. Decision to follow hampers choice. "Not my will, but Thine be done" is ever the compliance of the disciple. The Lord Jesus Christ was born with every faculty. No purpose of His could be restrained. All authority in heaven and earth was His. He chose to do His Father's will. His words were not His, but God's who sent Him.

His daily guidance was meted out to Him as He waited upon His God. "My food is to do the will of Him who sent Me" (Jn.4:34). "I can do nothing on My own initiative ... because I do not seek My own will, but the will of Him who sent Me" (Jn.5:30; 6:38). "My teaching is not Mine", He said (Jn.7:16). "As the Father hath said unto me, so I speak" (Jn.12:50 RV). Originally a choice had been made: "... just as He chose us in Him before the foundation of the world ... He pre-destined us to adoption as sons" (Eph.1:4,5). Once that choice had been made there followed full commitment in harmony with it. Come back now to the words of Joshua, or Elijah: Can I do less than obey, serve, exult, in the choice that God has made for me? "For even Christ did not please Himself" (Rom.15:3).

CHAPTER THIRTY-FOUR: ON THE THRONE - GOD'S SOVEREIGNTY OVER THE NATIONS

Someone has noticed that the book of Isaiah resembles a Bible in miniature. Its 66 chapters are divided, as Scripture is, into 39 and 27; the first segment centres around Israel's failure under the law, and the second, Israel's future glory through grace.

Judgement accompanies failure to measure up to the demands of God. This was true not only of those under the law, but the nations around about them of whom God had certain righteous expectations demanded because God had revealed His requirements to all men (Rom.1:18-20). Isaiah 40:15-17 places the nations of the earth in divine perspective: In God's view the nations are as a drop in the bucket, as the small dust on the balance, as less than nothing and vanity. Contrasted with this the people of God are viewed as a chosen people, His own special people, a holy nation, whether under the old covenant (Deut.10:14,15) or under the new (1 Pet.2:9). Nevertheless, Isaiah's detailed burdens regarding many nations show clearly that God has a keen interest in other nations and a control of their destinies, particularly those directly affecting His people. God is a God of universal sovereignty, affording blessing upon those who fear Him, and justice on those who don't.

But God was merciful to peoples and clans that were subdued by Israel. Under David, the Cherethites, Pelethites and Gittites who were content to bow to the God of Israel found a place of service among His people. Nations at odds with Israel and with God do have an opportunity to change. God remains merciful, accepting the repentant, whether nations or individuals, but His Spirit will not strive with either forever. God had chosen Israel, a nation for His own possession, and the same applies under the new covenant also and pours blessing upon those who are in His holy nation today. We were once no people, but now are the people of God.

The song of Moses in Deuteronomy 32:8 gives the picture of Israel's position: "When the Most High gave the nations their inheritance, when He separated the sons of men, He set the boundaries of the peoples according to the number of the sons of Israel. For the Lord's portion is His people ..." (NASB). All other nations were bounded and controlled by the interest God had in His own. Moses conveyed God's promise: "Now it shall come to pass, if you diligently obey the voice of the LORD your God ... the LORD your God will set you high above all nations of the earth" (Deut.28:1). However, the opposite was also true and on occasion God raised up other nations to bring judgement upon Israel because of their obstinacy, but woe to the nation that went beyond the parameters afforded it or which carried out its responsibilities with cruelty.

God's promise to Abraham that He would bless those who blessed him and curse those who cursed him applied also to the great people that God would make of him (Gen.12:3). Transgressing nations must come under judgement themselves oftentimes at the hands of other nations also destined for judgement. Even those nations carrying out that judgement must not exceed the task given to them, under threat of like punishment.

Amos 2:1 shows that even nations used to judge enemy nations must not go beyond the frame of reference given to them: for burning the bones of the king of Edom, Moab and its citadels would be consumed. Those bent on the destruction of the apple of God's eye must themselves be annihilated.

The question of how a righteous God could use those more wicked than Israel to punish their sins is one of the main concerns of Habakkuk who also wrote prior to Nebuchadnezzar's captivity of Judah. The answer is found in chapter 2 of his book: God was righteous, and His promise concerning Israel was sure. A nation like Babylon might be used for judgement, but any movement beyond her call would be likewise judged. Sometimes a nation not only embodied the philosophy that might is right, but carried it to the extent that the expression of such might was necessarily divine (Is.36:10). In this they exceeded all bounds, and as Amos had promised destruction to Damascus, Philistia, Tyre, Edom, Ammon and Moab, Babylon also must meet her destruction.

Isaiah added Assyria, Ethiopia, Egypt and Arabia to the list and included, as did Amos, Israel and Judah. In most, if not all cases, the message given concerning other nations was for Israel to hear rather than the offending peoples. God's covenanted people got the message that arrogance would not be tolerated and the enemies of God's people were God's enemies and would be dispatched as such. Israel herself must not exercise pride or cruelty, and because she had done, her punishment was imminent. Part of the difficulty in understanding when the prophesied destruction was to occur is that Isaiah includes impending devastation under the Assyrian hordes and God's final disposition of the nations prior to and at the return to earth of the Lord in end times. Scripture here, as elsewhere, has a double fulfilment. Assyria was to destroy many nations in Isaiah's immediate future (10:7). And because the axe boasted over the one who chopped with it (10:15), it too must be burnt up.

Isaiah's prophecy against Gentile nations started in the east at Babylon and worked westward before finishing up at Tyre. From the time of the tower in the plain of Shinar, Babylon has been characterized by disobedience, rebellion and hatred towards God, so much so, that all who engender such rebellion are seen as Babylon. Even in the future, religious and commercial Babylon will be considered great, but will fall under the mighty hand of the One who protects His people (Rev.17,18). Total destruction of all that pertains to her relentless disobedience against God will be fulfilled as prophesied by John in Revelation.

But God did not hate the other cities and nations just because they were not of Israel. Had they lived righteously according to the measure of knowledge afforded them they would have enjoyed a blessing from the LORD. The nations in question served other gods and were a snare to the people of the one true God (Ex.20:3; 23:33). The pattern still exists: our world is full of idols which are a snare and a delusion, affecting not only our testimony but the extent of our eternal reward. Such shall know the righteous judgement of a God who still protects His people. Satan's influence, perverting any right that any country might attempt, will also bring judgement from God upon that great enemy. Isaiah 14 shows the result of pride upon one who said in his heart, "I will ascend to heaven ... I will make myself like the Most High" (vv.13,14 NASB).

Paul shows the opposite attitude in Christ in Philippians 2:5 where the epitome of humility is seen in One who, although He existed in the form of God, did not regard equality with God a thing to be grasped, but emptied Himself. The godly will have a similar attitude. Isaiah 14:17 shows the character of Satan: He is ever occupied in taking prisoners. The opposite is seen in the Saviour who proclaimed release to the captives and freedom to the downtrodden (Lk.4:18). Though desolation is predicted by Isaiah in such chapters as 13 to 23, there are bright shining promises that he also brought to the people. God's people would outlast her judgements and be returned in glory to her land (Is.14:1). The LORD would bring rest after pain, turmoil and harsh service. The God who inscribed Zion upon the palms of His hands had her well-being ever before Him (Is.49:16). Not only will Israel be blessed in that future day, but Egypt and Assyria with her will share in millennial blessings, having bowed the knee to the Lord and by living in peace with each other (Is.19:16-25). Those nations refusing to do so will perish.

Gentiles who have become Christian believers through faith in Christ and His finished work at Calvary must ever be thankful that we who were at one time separated from Christ, excluded from the commonwealth of Israel, and strangers from the covenants of promise, having no hope and without God in the world have been brought near by the blood of Christ. And those rejoicing in the house of God, in covenant relationship with God through Him who has been raised from the dead with the blood of an eternal covenant, need to be doubly thankful. We are no longer strangers and aliens, but are fellow citizens with the saints and are of God's household. No longer among nations which must perish, we have all the promises of God just waiting to be revealed. We share in the gracious promises of the second segment of Isaiah's "grand measure".

CHAPTER THIRTY-FIVE: WHY THE EXCITEMENT?

The queen of Sheba could have found much in the kingdom of Solomon to be ecstatic about (1 Kin.10; 2 Chr.9). Silver and gold were as plenteous as stones in the capital (2 Chr.1:15); a gold-covered ivory throne with lions on either side, unlike any other throne on earth (2 Chr.9:17-19) and hundreds of shields of beaten gold adorned his palace. The land abounded with working animals, chariot horses, apes and peacocks, spices and riches. Even Solomon's palanquin, and the cedar and exotic woods, the extent of the kingdom and its place at the head of the nations might all have excited her.

But she became breathless when she considered Solomon's wisdom, the food of his table, the attire of his retinue, and his staircase. Perhaps she was moved by all she saw. Why then did the Spirit of God include a few seemingly inconsequential matters, food, clothing, a staircase, as the root of her wonder? There is no doubt that Solomon's kingdom prefigures the millennial triumph of the Lord, but there is significance for us to meditate on, even in a few simple elements for today. A greater than Solomon is here.

Can any but wonder at the One in whom all the treasures of wisdom and knowledge are hidden? Christ is the wisdom of God. In every sense He is the effulgence of the manifold wisdom of Deity, the embodiment of what James describes as the wisdom that is from above. We adore Him now; we shall yet admit that the half has not been told. Sheba's queen found amazement in the seating and attire of servants. And we have more cause to sit in wonder as we meditate upon the grace of God in seating us with him in the heavenly places in Christ, that in the ages to come He might show the surpassing riches of His grace in kindness toward us in Christ Jesus.

And if their attire was marvellous, what of the clothing in which we are now seen, perfected by Him who made the lilies of the field with a beauty which even Solomon in all His glory could not display? We are clothed with robes of righteousness, the like of which Israel was promised only in millennial splendour, in garments of salvation (Is.61:10). And what of our future? We are invited today to buy of Him robes of fine linen white and pure, and be dressed as overcomers in the day when we shall see and be with Him (Rev.3:5,18).

And Solomon's ascent to the house of God, how can that compare with the way into His presence that His people now know? For we "are a chosen race, a royal priesthood, a holy nation, a people for God's own possession ..." (1 Pet.2:1 NASB). And we have confidence to enter the holy place by the blood of Jesus, by the new and living way He inaugurated for us (Heb.10:19).

Consider, too, the food of His table. Broken bread, a poured-out cup of wine, leading to the remembrance of Christ and the showing forth to God of the excellencies of Him who called us. The queen of Sheba may have been confounded by the many things she saw. The Holy Spirit records a few which we also can meditate upon with wonder.

CHAPTER THIRTY-SIX: GIVING TO GOD

In Genesis 43 Jacob suggested that his sons go back to Egypt for food and with them take a present to the lord of the land. Had he realized just who the lord was, what the eventual outcome would be, all that was involved in giving, would he have suggested a little balm, a little honey, a little anything? Would he not have given all that he had, himself included (1)? We are given the tremendous opportunity to give to the Lord of heaven, the one for whom, through whom and to whom are all things. Are we still fixated on a little?

Of those noble saints in Macedonia Paul records: "they first gave themselves to the Lord" (2). That is where giving to God must begin. Giving will not make a Christian more spiritual. Spirituality, however, may well lead to giving. And where spirituality is lacking, God has no use for conscience money, money given to make up for spiritual shortcomings. God does not need our money (3). The earth is the Lord's and all it contains (4). He gives us the opportunity to give so that He might abundantly bless us with more, both here and hereafter (5). "Give, and it will be given to you ... good measure - pressed down, shaken together, and running over. For by your standard of measure it will be measured to you in return" (6).

Scripture gives some very practical guidelines about giving to God. Here are a few: Poverty is not an excuse not to give. Again the Macedonian churches are cited as examples: "... their deep poverty overflowed in the wealth of their liberality" (7). And the poor widow who gave so generously to the treasury as the Lord looked on, stands out as a shining example to us all (8). The Lord still watches the treasury! Nevertheless, Scripture also teaches balance in the matter. A person should not go into debt in order to give to God. Paul teaches clearly that "... it is acceptable according to what a person has, not according to what he does not have" (9). He also makes clear that giving is to be as a person may prosper (10). But we are often amazed how prosperity follows that initial giving. God remains debtor to no one.

Another of the guidelines discusses our attitude in giving. God loves a cheerful giver (11). This goes along with the willing spirit that God so desires. In the Old Testament Israel met the standard: Then the people rejoiced because they had offered so willingly, for they made their offering to the LORD with a whole heart, and King David also rejoiced greatly (12).

1 Chronicles 29 has several pertinent things to say about the subject at hand. Verse 12: "Both riches and honour come from You ... and it lies in Your hand to make great and to strengthen everyone." Verse 14: "Who am I and who are my people that we should be able to offer as generously as this? For all things come from You, and from Your hand we have given You." God gives; we are blessed; and then we are doubly blessed in giving. In the New Testament, Paul rejoiced when individuals and churches rose to their God-given responsibilities (13). And in both Old and New Testaments God was well-pleased.

God also leaves instruction that privacy should be a motivating factor in our generosity. "Beware of practising your righteousness before men to be noticed by them; otherwise you have no reward with your Father who is in heaven." The Lord Jesus then spoke on and in the next few verses Matthew records for us just how that is to affect our giving. Notice that the Lord does not say, 'if' you give in these verses, but 'when' you give, and He uses the often quoted phrase "do not let your left hand know what your right hand is doing" and finishes by stating,

"... your giving will be in secret; and your Father who sees what is done in secret will reward you" (14).

Tied in with this is also the subject of humility in giving. When Israel offered their first fruits the offerers came in remembrance of where they had originated, the hole of the pit from whence they had been extricated, expressed their thankfulness at the beneficence of God, and in worship presented their physical bounty and their spiritual sacrifices as well, rejoicing in their God-given ability to give (15).

Notice that what they were commanded to bring was the tithe, ten per cent of their prosperity. While we are not so bound in this day of grace, that commandment was never rescinded. Our joy should be that we are not limited to the tithe, and any restrictions of income tax laws and benefits should not enter the equation at all.

Another matter that this portion brings to our attention is that giving to God should be of the first fruits of His bounty to us, not the leftovers when all else has been cared for. A brilliant example of God's way of doing things is seen in 1 Kings 17:7-14. A widow with little to give and in great distress is asked first to supply to God's prophet, Elisha, the last morsel that she possessed. Her faithfulness in doing so was rewarded by God, her jar of oil and bowl of flour not failing until the famine that plagued the land had subsided. Honor the LORD from your wealth and from the first of all your produce; so your barns will be filled with plenty and your vats will overflow with new wine (16).

It is probably true in your case, as in mine, that there are those in our churches with deeper pockets and bigger hearts than we have, and perhaps seemingly fewer fiscal problems. That should in no way influence the subject of our giving. We are not called upon to sit back and let others do what is necessary. We are to do our part, however that compares with what others may give.

Now this I say, writes Paul, "he who sows sparingly will also reap sparingly, and he who sows bountifully will also reap bountifully" (17). The God who knows all about bountiful giving also knows all about bountiful rewarding. As in our secular handling of finance, we will probably find that systematic giving is helpful in keeping us on track. Paul instructed the Corinthians to weekly set aside their givings, saving them for the appropriate time, as the Lord prospered them (18). Some orderly method of giving might also assist us in our striving to please the One who gave so freely for us.

Some practical lessons might be taken from the financial business world. The use of credit cards and bank debit cards has mushroomed in recent years, so that in some areas there is practically a cashless society. The fact is when we use a credit card we are for the moment spending someone else's money, and somehow we have less difficulty doing that than spending our own. We need to ask ourselves whose money we are handling anyway.

We get used to thinking of _my_ pay cheque, _my_ pocket money, _my_ bank account, when we should realize that whatever possessions that we handle are only in our hands because they have been placed under our stewardship. "What do you have that you did not receive?" asks Paul. "And if you did receive it, why do you boast as if you had not received it?" (19). Moses said, "Otherwise, you may say in your heart, 'My power and the strength of my hand made me this wealth.' But you shall remember the LORD your God, for it is He who is giving you power to make wealth" (20). It is true that control of that wealth is in our hands meantime, but so is the responsibility to disperse it to the glory of God (21). The talent hidden in the handkerchief receives no reward; indeed, the mishandling of the Lord's money brings judgment (22).

Paul points out that anything done without love as the motivator is valueless in the sight of God (23). Someone has also added that it is possible to give without love, but it is impossible to love without giving. Pursue love (24)! Both Matthew and Luke quoted Christ: "... you cannot serve God and wealth" (25). But we can serve God with our money. The Lord also said, "It is more blessed to give than to receive" (26). The sheer number of scriptures on this subject of giving should waken us to greater responsibility!

Herbert Lockyer tells the story of the prosperous farmer who was questioned by his neighbours about how he could give so freely, yet always have more to give. His response was that the answer was easy. "I keep shovelling into God's barn and He keeps shovelling into mine. He has the bigger shovel!"

References: (1) Gen.46:1 (2) 2 Cor.8:5 (3) Ps.50:12 (4) Ps.24:1 (5) Mal.3:10 (6) Lk.6:38 (7) 2 Cor.8:2 (8) Mk.12:43-44 (9) 2 Cor.8:12 (10) 1 Cor.16:2 (11) 2 Cor.9:7 (12) 1 Chron.29:9 (13) 2 Cor.8:2; Phil.4:16-18 (14) Matt.6:1-4 (15) Deut.26:1-17 (16) Prov.3:9-10 (17) 2 Cor.9:6 (18) 1 Cor.16:1-2 (19) 1 Cor.4:7 (20) Deut.8:17-18 (21) Acts 5:4 (22) Lk.19:20,26 (23) 1 Cor.13:1-3 (24) 1 Cor.14:1 (25) Matt.6:24; Lk.16:13 (26) Acts 20:35

CHAPTER THIRTY-SEVEN: BETHLEHEM

―――

"But you Bethlehem Ephrathah, though you are little among the thousands of Judah, yet out of you shall come forth to Me the One to be Ruler in Israel, Whose goings forth are from of old, from everlasting" (Mic.5:2).

We read little in Scripture about the town of Bethlehem. That it was small is apparent in Micah's description; it was on a hill and defensible, for in David's day the Philistines had a garrison there. There was also a well of sweet water in it. From its name, the house of bread, and from the description of Boaz's harvest (Ruth 2:3) we learn that its fields were fruitful. The hillsides around were suitable for raising sheep. its most important product were the men who came from there, and though little is also said about them, what is recorded is poignant pointing forward to the One who would come from the town unto God, to be Ruler in Israel, whose goings forth are from old, from everlasting.

Benjamin was born on Bethlehem's outskirts. Not much is reported about his life, but in several outstanding ways he is a shadow of the One to come. As a young man he accompanied his ten older brothers to Egypt to obtain supplies. He was arrested on his return journey when a cup was found in his bag. He, though innocent, must pay the penalty, while the ten sinful brothers might have gone free, and that, with treasure in their sacks. The picture comes into focus when we consider Christ's words: "Shall I not drink the cup which My Father has given Me?" (Jn.18:11). Asaph wrote about a cup in the hands of the Lord, full and foaming and to be poured out that the wicked of the earth might drink it. Christ drank the cup of judgement that we, the wicked, might go free, and that with unspeakable treasure, here and hereafter.

Not much is written about Ibzan of Bethlehem. He judged Israel for seven years. He sired thirty sons and thirty daughters. and multiplied their number in marriage. Why should the Spirit cause that sort of detail to be recorded? Then we remember that he also was a foreshadow of another from Bethlehem of whom Isaiah wrote: "I and the children whom the LORD has given me!" (Is.8:18). And we rejoice to be counted among those children (Heb.2:13), and not only so, but to be seen as sons and daughters (2 Cor.6:18), who because of Christ can manifest characteristics of the Father, partakers of the divine nature (2 Pet.1.4).

The fruitfulness of the fields of Boaz became more precious when it was laden freely upon Ruth, the one who would one day possess the whole treasure that was his. He not only was chosen as part of the royal lineage, he also displayed the liberality of the Redeemer. Ruth's life gradually became full of the blessings of the LORD. We, like Ruth, are daily showered with His blessings and are awaiting the whole harvest.

David was born in Bethlehem, the man after God's own heart, the shepherd who was to save Israel and become king. He speaks to us of the Shepherd who not only risked, but gave His life for the sheep, who Himself shall one day be displayed as KING OF KINGS AND LORD OF LORDS (Rev.19:16), who shall reign forever and forever.

The men of Bethlehem pointed forward to the Man of Bethlehem, who a few short miles from there became the Man of Calvary. He is the source of fruitfulness. He is the well of Bethlehem, of which, if a man drink, he shall live forever. It was water from the well at Bethlehem that David would not drink because His mighty men had risked their lives to obtain it. He "poured it out to the LORD" (1 Chr.11:17-19). The Man of Calvary was also "poured out like water" as an offering to the LORD (Ps.22:14). The Victor of Calvary has become our high hill, our strong tower. We know that: "The name of the LORD is a strong tower: the righteous run into it and are safe" (Prov.18:10).

"His goings forth are from of old, from everlasting" and our goings forth with Him shall be to everlasting. Meantime, the green pastures and still waters attest to the care of the One who has become the "Shepherd and Overseer of our souls" (1 Pet.2:25). Praise God for what came out of Bethlehem.

Did you love *Called As We Are*? Then you should read *The View From Goak Hill: A Christian's Perspective on Life and Living*[1] by Gilbert Grierson!

[2]

Gilbert's life changed when he came to know Jesus in Israel in 1975: "God opened my eyes to see truth that brought me peace and hope. Now I look at the world differently. These writings are my attempt to pass on what I see from my "Goak Hill" to ordinary people like myself who are troubled about the world we live in and are looking for answers".

A potter and former hospice nurse, Gilbert combines Bible verses and some of his everyday experiences to draw out some challenging and encouraging life lessons for a journey through life with Jesus.

---

1. https://books2read.com/u/bWVXz4

2. https://books2read.com/u/bWVXz4

Also by Ed Neely

Called As We Are

About the Publisher

Hayes Press (www.hayespress.org) is a registered charity in the United Kingdom, whose primary mission is to disseminate the Word of God, mainly through literature. It is one of the largest distributors of gospel tracts and leaflets in the United Kingdom, with over 100 titles and hundreds of thousands despatched annually. In addition to paperbacks and eBooks, Hayes Press also publishes Plus Eagles Wings, a fun and educational Bible magazine for children, and Golden Bells, a popular daily Bible reading calendar in wall or desk formats. Also available are over 100 Bibles in many different versions, shapes and sizes, Bible text posters and much more!

www.ingramcontent.com/pod-product-compliance
Lightning Source LLC
Chambersburg PA
CBHW031357040426
42444CB00005B/327